MW01100434

THE JOURNAL OF THE BLACK CATHOLIC THEOLOGICAL SYMPOSIUM (BCTS), was founded in 2007.

MANUSCRIPTS, based on talks originally delivered at the Annual Meetings of the BCTS, should be submitted to the editorial board shortly after the Annual Meeting ends. They should be formatted in Chicago Turabian style with Works Cited page and sent via electronic mail to the editor-in-chief, Cyprian Davis, O.S.B.: CDavis@saintmeinrad.edu, and also to senior editor Kimberly Flint-Hamilton: kflintha@stetson.edu. A hard copy of the manuscript should be mailed to: Kimberly Flint-Hamilton, Department of Sociology and Anthropology, Unit 8387, Stetson University, 421 North Woodland Blvd, Deland, FL, 32723. For examples of Chicago Turabian style, see: http://www.lib.berkeley.edu/instruct/guides/chicago-turabianstyle.pdf

Contributors must submit original work. The Journal of the Black Catholic Theological Symposium is composed of original articles by its members, and will not publish manuscripts that have been previously published elsewhere.

REVIEWS of books or films that have relevance to the Black Catholic Theological Symposium may also be submitted and will be considered for publication. Reviews originally published elsewhere will not be considered for publication.

MEMBERSHIP in the Black Catholic Theological Symposium is by invitation only. Those interested in joining the organization may review membership guidelines from Article II of the Constitution, posted on the BCTS web site: http://www.bcts.org, and contact the secretary of the BCTS, Shawnee Daniels-Sykes, SSND, at the following electronic mail address: sykess@mtmary.edu.

The opinions expressed in the articles and/or reviews published in the Journal of the Black Catholic Theological Symposium are those of the authors and are not necessarily the opinions of the editorial board, the organization, or the publisher.

The Journal of the Black Catholic Theological Symposium is provided to all paid members of the BCTS. Additional copies of the journal may be obtained by contacting the publisher, Steven Hamilton, of Fortuity Press, at the following electronic mail address: steven.hamilton@fortuitypress.com.

Fortuity Press

Printed in the United States of America.
Cover design by Kimberly Flint-Hamilton, Steven Hamilton
Interior design by Kimberly Flint-Hamilton, Steven Hamilton

THE JOURNAL

OF THE

BLACK CATHOLIC THEOLOGICAL SYMPOSIUM (BCTS)

VOLUME THREE

THE BLACK CATHOLIC THEOLOGICAL SYMPOSIUM (BCTS)

2009 OFFICERS

Bryan Massingale, Convener

C. Vanessa White, Associate Convener

Shawnee Daniels-Sykes, S.S.N.D., Secretary

Robert Bartlett, Treasurer

Cyprian Davis, O.S.B., Archivist

Kimberly Flint-Hamilton, Past Convener

THE JOURNAL OF THE BCTS

Volume Three October 2009

A Year of Extremes

Kimberly Flint-Hamilton, Senior Editor
Stetson University

2009 – what an incredible year! A year of almost inconceivable highs, and lows that bore down into our very beings, the time since we met last October has filled us with high hopes as well as dark fears. These conflicted realities are reflected both in our lives and in our work.

For most BCTS members, indeed, for most Americans, the election of our first African American president was one of the most significant moments of our lives. I'll never forget when Obama was declared victor shortly after 11:00 pm EST on November 4, 2008. As late as it was, I picked up the telephone and called my close friends, many of whom were in tears when they answered. We were ecstatic, and wondered to ourselves if this just might be the signal that the U.S. heritage of structured, entrenched racism was beginning to fade away. It didn't take long for us to find out that the face of racism may have changed, but it was far from gone.

I remember racing home from campus on that cold January Inauguration Day so I could tune in to the network coverage of the Inauguration ceremonies. I was so eager to share in the fanfare that I even checked the White House web site for the lunch menu. I imagined the way the room looked as various gourmet dishes were brought out to our first black

President and his First Lady. I prayed for Senator Ted Kennedy when he collapsed midway through lunch, and I prayed even harder that Obama wouldn't collapse next, so fearful was I of nefarious intrigue by racist congressional insiders. It was an afternoon of highs and lows, and I stayed tuned into the coverage until the new President and First Lady graced the ballroom floor for the first presidential dance. I felt like I was a part of those events in a way I never have before.

Yet, not long after Obama took office, we saw the U.S. economy come crashing down, a process that began long before the election. It continued to plunge as we saw the highest unemployment figures for decades, the worst recession since the Great Depression, with many insisting we were actually in a depression. It felt like a depression to many Americans as we struggled to make ends meet after we and/or our spouses were laid off. And as our academic institutions tightened their belts, reduced operating budgets, withdrew funds for travel and research, and sent pink slips to 'nonessential personnel', we all shuddered. The Tea Partiers objected to big government spending even as the economy began to improve, and the Birthers called Obama's citizenship into question despite birth notices in a 1961 Hawaiian newspaper and a copy of his U.S. birth certificate. While all that was going on, the nation reaffirmed our aversion to torture and the Guantanomo detainees began to be released. In the same election that ended with Obama victorious, some states banned same-sex marriage while others overturned existing laws allowing it, thereby robbing GLBT couples of a little piece of their humanity. Senator Kennedy passed away, and the health care debate rages on without him as the fate of the uninsured and underinsured swings in the balance. This has been quite a year.

The drama of this past year is reflected in Volume III of *The Journal of the BCTS.* Our contributors take a bold look at some of the most controversial issues of the world today, and challenge the comfort zone of Catholic scholars, even many black Catholic scholars. This volume focuses on the margins of the marginalized. Ken Hamilton, SVD challenges the Church's assumptions of a heteronormative sexual identity and shows us that demonization of 'othered' identities as evil have contributed to the suffering of AIDS victims. Daniels-Sykes explores the medical atrocities that lead to the 1979 Belmont Report, and describes the ways in which it fostered a bioethics that relies on the presumption "normativity of whiteness," and thereby failing to consider the ways in which whites are privileged at the expense of blacks. She posits a black Catholic liberation bioethics that is responsive to the needs of blacks. Finally, James Okoye, CSSp describes the ways in which African women interpret the Bible alongside other religious texts and traditions to better understand their lived experiences as a marginalized group. We also include three book reviews – Tim Wise's *Between Barack and a Hard Plac*e (2009), which presents the new face of racism in the post-Obama era; the controversial Clarence Thomas' *My Grandfather's Son: A Memoir* (2007), which reveals the struggles of a former Catholic and his quest for identity; and *Uncommon Faithfulness: The Black Catholic Experience*, edited by M. Shawn Copeland with LaReine-Marie Mosely, SND, and Albert Raboteau, which features articles by several of our members that seek to illuminate the many ways in which our faith has been revealed and articulated from the time of slavery to the present. Volume III of *The Journal of the BCTS* is the most groundbreaking issue yet. The reader is guaranteed not to be disappointed!

What A Difference A Year Makes

Cecilia Moore, Editor
University of Dayton

I'd like to reflect briefly on the election of President Barack Obama and Vice-President Joseph Biden in 2008 and their inauguration in January 2009, on the historical significance of the election, and my hopes for cooperation between the Black Catholic community and the Obama Administration in working for social justice.

On January 20, 2009, I joined my sister, Margaret, my brother, Mark, and a million or more of our fellow citizens on the nation's Mall to witness the inauguration of President Barack Obama and Vice-President Joseph Biden. In freezing temperatures, without access to restrooms for more than 14 hours, and with scant opportunities for food or water, we were on pilgrimage to help initiate what may become the most important presidency for the United States in recent times. My sister and I spent countless afternoons knocking on doors and canvassing voters in Virginia and Ohio. We got to know our respective cities, Danville, Virginia and Dayton, Ohio, so much better and became adept users of Google maps and canvass abbreviations. We learned more about the political process, especially about the differences between primaries and caucuses, super delegates and regular delegates, and key political players in our own localities. We engaged in community organization. We became addicted to the *Huffington Post* and *Politico* and major fans of Rachel Maddow. Each day we felt more hopeful about the promise of our generation to do something truly positive for the common good.

At school, people knew about my commitment to the Obama campaign. Over the course of the campaign, I worked with many friends from the University of Dayton in various Dayton neighborhoods and in the surrounding suburbs on canvassing and getting out the vote during the Ohio primary and in the general election in November. I spent election eve at a "First Vote Party" for undergraduates that was hosted by faculty. I was thrilled, as were my faculty friends at the "First Vote Party," when Ohio was solidly added to the Obama/Biden column. I was sure we would go for Obama in Ohio but I really wanted the victory for Virginia. I saved my biggest cheer for when Virginia went blue. The next day, I was especially happy to see a tiny dot of blue in the sea of red that was Pittsylvania County. That tiny dot was the final home of the Confederacy, the site of the Wreck of the Old '97, the birthplace of Lady Astor, Camilla Williams, and Wendell Scott, and a primary battleground of the civil rights movement. That tiny dot was Danville, Virginia going for Obama by 59%. This victory signaled two things. First it showed that a town that for generations reveled in its Confederate history and heritage was ready and willing to assist in bringing forth the first president of African descent of the United States. The second thing the Danville victory showed was that the tradition of political activism fostered by generations of African American religious leaders in Danville still had the power to make things happen. My sister told me how proud she felt to be at her poll on Election Day and to see so many generations of African Americans there to vote. Many could remember people in their own families who never got to exercise this privilege and responsibility. And, many also never dreamed that they would have the opportunity to vote for an African American for president. It was a time ripe with the fulfillment of things long hoped for. Simply put, it was a wonderful year and we felt very good about all the work we and millions more had done to make that day come. The physical hardships January 20 presented in Washington, D.C. were small prices to pay for the privilege to be there in person for the inauguration.

So much has happened since. When one thinks about it, we have our first Black and Catholic White House. Our president is Black and he credits Catholic community activists in Chicago with helping to form his sense of social justice and his commitment to pursuing it. Our vice-president is a Roman Catholic who seems to have a real voice and influence in the White House. Blacks and Catholics are serving in President Obama's cabinet and on his staff. The appointment of Dr. Miguel Diaz as the United States Ambassador to the Holy See this past August is an important example of President Obama making good on his promise of "change you can believe in" with his nomination of the first theologian and the first Latino serve this important diplomatic post. Ambassador Diaz is a past president of the Academy of Catholic Hispanic Theologians in the United States. He has shown his commitment to building and strengthening the relationships of Latino/a Catholic and Black Catholic theologians and

..unities of faith. In 2006, he invited the Black Catholic Theological Symposium to meet in *cojunto* with ACHTUS.

President Obama thinks religion has an important role to play in the public square and in contributing to the common good. He has maintained a strong relationship with representatives of various faith communities in the United States and continues to seek their advice in how best to address social, economic, health, and moral issues that concern all of us. After so many years of religion being used as a political weapon in the public square, these new changes are really refreshing. It is a new day that presents us in the Black Catholic Theological Symposium and in the wider Black Catholic community with many opportunities to offer our gifts, time, energy, creativity, experiences, constructive criticism, scholarship and concerns to the service of our country. Concerns that members of the BCTS have been addressing in our scholarship, teaching, and work in our parishes and faith communities for years are on the agenda of this White House. We have a special opportunity now to help bring about changes in our society that will particularly serve the best interests of our many brothers and sisters who have suffered for such a long time. Our president is calling us to help make health care reform a reality in our day, to recommit ourselves to making education work to its fullest potential for our children, and to get involved in our local communities to address the problems and needs of our neighbors. It is my hope that we can transform the passion that so many of us had during the election last year to lend our hands, our minds, and our hearts to the magnificent mission that is presented to us now.

Voices from the Margins: African Women's Hermeneutics

James Chukwuma Okoye, C.S.Sp.
Catholic Theological Union

In this article delivered during the 2008 Annual Meeting in Chicago, Okoye describes several landmarks in African biblical interpretation from the various lenses of race, class, and gender. From the early days of a culturally-sensitive African hermeneutics in the 1960s, to modern popular readings of the Bible, to women's unique readings of the shades of meaning therein, Okoye focus on the intersection points of biblical and cultural interpretation and the ways a marginalized people have found meaning in the Bible.

Luke 12:31 reads as follows: "no; set your hearts on [God's] kingdom, and these other things will be given you as well" (*New Jerusalem Bible*). Brian Blount chose this text for a youth Bible study, a text that always gives him spiritual upliftment as it promises reward in the end after a disciplined existence of delayed gratification. He was taken aback when the text met with violent resistance from one of the young girls. She was appalled that it counseled leaving everything to God rather than a concerted human effort to transform her reality of constant deprivation.[1] "Every reading bears the stamp of who reads."[2]

Since 1970 a plethora of approaches is being used in biblical interpretation. An emerging factor is the shift away from the translation model (coding—decoding, "what it meant"—"what it means"). Current theories tend to focus on the ongoing dialogue of text and reader. African readings bear the stamp of the African context and culture. Hermeneutics has proven to be a sharp tool for liberation, racial liberation in South Africa under apartheid and cultural and gender liberation for African women in their double struggle with culture and Bible/church.

1. Landmarks in Biblical Interpretation in Africa

In the Conference of Berlin, 1885, the then-European powers took out a map of Africa and carved it up among themselves. Between 1930 and 1950 several nationalistic movements began to dot the map of Africa; the spirit of *négritude* promoted by Senghor[3] was in the air. Ghana (formerly Gold Coast) became "independent" in 1956, the first African nation to throw off the British colonial yoke. 1956

---

[1] Brian K. Blount, *Cultural Interpretation: Reorienting New Testament Criticism* (Minneapolis: Fortress Press, 1995), 1.

[2] Mary Ann Tolbert, "The Politics and Poetics of Location," in *Reading From This Place. Volume 1: Social Location and Biblical Interpretation in the United States,* ed. Fernando Segovia and Mary Ann Tolbert (Minneapolis, MN: Fortress Press, 1995) 305-317, here 314.

[3] Leopold Senghor was elected president of Senegal in the 1960s, and retired from office in 1980. Poet as well as politician, Senghor's concept of 'negritude' encompassed the artistic and literary expression of the Black African experience.

also saw the first Congress of Negro Writers and Artists in Paris. Between 1956 and 1975 most African nations regained independence, except Zimbabwe and South Africa. Now began the immense task of retrieving African identity and culture.

The first recent attempt to develop a culturally sensitive hermeneutics in Africa was, to my knowledge, the first Consultation of African Theologians on *Bible and Africa* which met at Ibadan, Nigeria in 1965; it was published as *Biblical Revelation and African Beliefs*.[4] The method was mostly that of comparative hermeneutics. Then in 1970 the Black Theology Seminar at Wilgespruit, South Africa was greatly influenced by James Cone and his *Black Theology and Black Power* published the previous year. From this seminar emerged the South African black theology of liberation, one of the forces that brought down the apartheid regime. Political hermeneutics of liberation in South Africa used to be contrasted with African inculturation theology in the rest of sub-Saharan Africa, but post-apartheid South Africa is rediscovering culture as a factor in hermeneutics, while sub-Saharan Africa has been developing various forms of liberation hermeneutics.

In 1975 the West African Association of Theological Institutions (WAATI) planned Bible commentaries to look afresh at the Bible from an African perspective and relate biblical interpretation to life situations in Africa. For financial

---

[4] Kwesi Dickson and Paul Ellingworth, eds. *Biblical Revelation and African Beliefs* (London: Lutherworth Press, 1969).

reasons the project barely got off the ground before dying with the death of the general editor, Fashole-Luke, in 1991. The next significant contribution to hermeneutics in Africa was the Kairos Document, *Challenge to the Church: A Theological Comment on the Political Situation in South Africa*, 1985.[5] The theologians who worked on this document challenged the type of hermeneutics that created apartheid, which dispossessed black people of their land and gave the better part of it to God's "chosen people," the white Boers. The Institute for the Study of the Bible, Natal was founded in 1990 and took on "reading with" ordinary readers as a favored project. A major landmark was the founding in 1989 of the *Circle of Concerned African Women Theologians* under the leadership of Mercy Amba Oduyoye of Ghana, henceforth The Circle. The Circle, barely ten of whose members are trained biblical academicians, has nevertheless been an important voice for African hermeneutics in general and African women's hermeneutics in particular. Its first hermeneutical input was, *Other Ways of Reading: African Women and the Bible*.[6] Ever since 1995 Mugambi has been advocating paradigms for political and social reconstruction based, not on Exodus but on the reconstruction program of Ezra-Nehemiah.[7] The University of Stellenbosch, South Africa began a database of the *Bible in Africa* in 1999; it currently has over 2000 entries. Some of this database appeared in *The Bible in Africa:*

---

[5] Second edition (Grand Rapids: Eerdmans, 1986).

[6] (Atlanta, GA: Society of Biblical Literature; Geneva: World Council of Churches, 2001).

[7] Jesse Kanyua Mugambi, *From Liberation to Reconstruction: African Christian Theology After the Cold War* (Nairobi, Kenya: East African Educational Publishers, 1995); *Christian Theology and Social Reconstruction*. (Nairobi: Acton Publishers, 2003).

Transactions, Trajectories and Trends, edited by Musa Dube and Gerald West.[8] This 800-page work contains almost 200 pages of bibliography of biblical interpretation in Africa and by Africans. Recently the one-volume, 1585 pages, *Africa Bible Commentary*[9] by the Association of Evangelicals of Africa (AEA) appeared. The seventy contributors were all African scholars and pastors: Anglicans, Baptists, Lutherans, Methodists, Presbyterians, Church of Christ, Pentecostals, ECWA,[10] AIC's, but naturally no Catholics. The policy states that the commentary should be African in authorship and content, and include issues affecting the continent. It should use African thought forms and practical applications that suit the African context. The contributors should be as diverse as the continent, including men and women, the various denominations and languages. They are also to work from the Hebrew and Greek originals and from translations into their mother tongue.

2. Popular Readings of the Bible in Africa

In the days of mission, "the Bible was very often the first and the only literature available to people in their own language."[11] Some of the older folk can still read nothing else but the Bible in the vernacular. Exegesis in the African cultural background remains predominantly oral, and is done

---

[8] (Leiden: E. J. Brill, 2000).

[9] Tokunboh Adeyemo, general editor (Nairobi, Kenya: WordAlive Publishers; Grand Rapids: Zondervan, 2006).

[10] Evangelical Church of West Africa.

[11] Wynnand Amewowo, "Experiences and Discoveries with the Bible in West Africa." *Mission Studies* 3/1 (1986): 12-24, here 14.

principally through sermons and drama. A sermon may use various artifices to interpret the text: e.g., repetition of verses with emphasis, songs, proverbs, stories either from the Bible or from culture and life. Drama generally interprets the text in the African perspective (see below).

Field studies on popular uses and interpretations of the Bible show that many regard the Bible as literally Word of God. In his research Justin Ukpong found that ordinary readers of the Bible have a dogmatic and reverential stance towards it. They do not approach it with a questioning mind, rather it serves for prayer and devotion and as norm for morality. He writes:

> They are interested neither in the literary analysis of the biblical texts nor in the history behind the text. They are interested in the theological message in the text and how that message might be useful to their lives.[12]

Spiritual churches use the Bible as well for healing and exorcism, and, partly for this reason, they are gaining many converts from the mainline churches. For them the Bible has a spiritual and universal meaning and is not subject to cultural interpretation.[13]

---

[12] *Ibid.*, 588.

[13] Justin Ukpong, "Popular Readings of the Bible in Africa and Implications for Academic Readings," in *The Bible in Africa: Transactions, Trajectories and Trends*, ed. Gerald O. West and Musa W. Dube (Leiden: E. J. Brill, 2001), 588.

Some accord the Bible magical powers, not unlike Muslim attitudes to the Quran.

> It is used to ward off spirits, witches and sorcerers; it is placed under the pillow at night to ensure God's protection against the devil, put in handbags and cars when traveling to ensure a safe journey, and used in swearing to bring God's wrath upon the culprits.[14]

An exegete[15] recounts how his father wrapped the Bible in white cloth and kept it under lock! It came out ceremonially for the swearing of oaths; hence it functioned like the *ọfọ* in Igbo traditional religion. The Cherubim and Seraphim and the Celestial Church of Christ have devised ritual uses of the Psalms[16] for protection, welfare and the fight against enemy forces. Such rituals are not unlike the use of traditional talismans. For example, Ps 109 is potent against enemies when recited in the middle of the night or at 1 p.m. in an open field, between three candles placed north, east and west, and read with the name of El, the name of the enemy, and the name of his/her mother in mind.

---

[14] Ukpong, "Popular Readings of the Bible in Africa," 587.

[15] Ernest Ezeogu, "Bible and Culture in African Christianity," *IRM* 87 (1998): 25-38, here 25.

[16] David Tuesday Adamo, "African Cultural Hermeneutics," in *Vernacular Hermeneutic,* ed. R. S. Sugirtharajah, (Sheffield: Sheffield Academic Press, 1999), 66-90, here 75.

Ukpong also notes that people generally read the Bible for individual benefit and that there was:

> lack of societal transformation as a motive for reading the bible … The bible is not read from the perspective of political or economic commitment.[17]

Several scholars are responding to this situation with programs of "reading with" orally educated folk. This practice, as far as I know, began around 1990 with Gerald O. West and the Institute for the Study of the Bible, University of Natal. His method has four elements: read from the perspective of the poor and marginalized, "read with," not listen to or speak for, relate the Bible to social transformation, and read the Bible critically.[18] Ukpong[19] and other African scholars[20] have also developed methods of "reading with." The goals and approaches are not always the same. For example, Musa Dube does not insist on critical apparatus nor

---

[17] Ukpong, "Popular Readings of the Bible in Africa," 591.

[18] Gerald O. West, "Reading the Bible Differently: Giving Shape to the Discourses of the Dominated," *Semeia* 73 (1996): 21-41, here 28. A workshop by West on Mark 5:21—6:1 is reported in his "Constructing Critical and Contextual Readings with Ordinary Readers," *Journal of Theology for South Africa* 92 (1997): 60-69. Another on Mark 10:17-22 is reported in *Neotestamentica* 27 (1993): 165-180.

[19] Getui, Mary, Tinyiko Maluleke, and Justin Ukpong, "Bible Reading with a Community of Ordinary Readers," in *Interpreting the New Testament in Africa,* ed. Mary Getui, Tinyiko Maluleke and Justin Ukpong (Nairobi, Kenya: Acton Publishers, 2001): 188-212: on Matt 20:1-16.

[20] Musimbi Kanyoro's work with Bware women (Kenya) on the book of Ruth will be reported later. See also Apheus Masoga, "Redefining Power: Reading the Bible in Africa from the Peripheral and Central Positions," in *Reading the Bible in the Global Village,* ed. Justin Ukpong, Musa Dube, Gerald West, et al. (Atlanta: SBL, 2001) 95-109: on John 5:1-10. Masoga advocates what he calls "conversational hermeneutic."

does she consciously goad readers towards social transformation; she only facilitates the process of interpretation with questions and merely records the people's own readings and approaches. I shall now examine two readings of the book of Ruth.

3. Hermeneutics of Resonance: Bware Women (Kenya) on Ruth

Musimbi Kanyoro held a three-day "theater of biblical hermeneutics" (as the women themselves called it) on the book of Ruth with 150 rural women of Bware village in Western Kenya.[21] They were to interpret the book through dramatization. The women were divided into five groups. The first would read the whole book and retell it in a story using their own words. The second group would present their interpretation of Naomi; the third would interpret Ruth, the fourth, Orpah. The fifth would retell the story of Ruth and Naomi back in Bethlehem after their return. After this facilitation Kanyoro left the women alone to interpret the story as they pleased. Here are salient features of their interpretation.

Mahlon and Chilion were punished with death because the family neglected their own customs for foreign ones. It may also be because they emigrated secretly leaving other kith and kin to suffer and someone in the family of Elimelech pronounced a curse against them. Perhaps they did not return

---

[21] Musimbi R. A. Kanyoro, "Biblical Hermeneutics: Ancient Palestine and the Contemporary World." *RevExp* 94 (1997): 363-378.

occasionally to pay homage to the dead and now suffered their curse. Ruth was the obedient and faithful daughter-in-law; her husband was a violent man who was mostly absent, and when present often beat her. Naomi was Ruth's refuge and consolation, so the two became very close friends. The two decided to return to Bethlehem maybe to offer sacrifice and ask the elders to cleanse the family. Boaz was rich and polygamous and that was why Ruth married him; he tricked the poorer man who should inherit Ruth.

Orpah was acted by a high school teacher who wore fashionable clothes. Split between cultural demands and a life on her own, she opted for the latter. While the other women poured scorn on her for being an educated rebel she stood her ground, but left alone on the stage she began to be confused and to cry saying, "could they be right? Should I have gone to Bethlehem with Ruth and my mother-in-law Naomi? Should I have gone to my parents?"[22] Then she ran off the stage. She later married a man of Moab and had children, but complained that "my story does not appear in the Bible, because Naomi never came back to visit me."

When asked what the story was about the women gave various answers. It was about the problems of refugees and the consequences of abandoning one's own customs. It was also about the problems of widows who have to fend for themselves. It was about inter-tribal marriages and accepting other tribes, about "wife-inheritance" (their term for biblical levirate marriage) and having good and responsible mothers-

---

[22] *Ibid.*, 374

in-law. They debated, and agreed to differ, about a wife's right to joint ownership of land and property. Some condemned polygamy, others justified it as part of culture.

A short reflection on the exegesis follows. The African conceptual framework underlies the hermeneutics above: themes of curse and witchcraft, the importance of adhering to tradition, and life as life in community. The women simply interpreted the text in terms of its resonance in their own culture, never asking the expert what the text meant. Hence, I characterize their hermeneutics as "*hermeneutics of resonance*." Their only concern was lest the church penalize them for being critical of any biblical character or adducing witchcraft as explanation for the many deaths, or for using cultural songs to present their interpretations. We can see that their church was loath to integrate faith and culture. But the women preserved the African concept of the unity of life whereby sacred and profane form one reality.

4. Divination Hermeneutics: Musa Dube on the Book of Ruth

The Bware women's critique of culture and Bible was inchoative; Musa Dube foregrounds such critique. She brings what she calls "divination hermeneutics"[23] to the study of this book. A divination session involves three parties: the divine powers, the diviner and the consulting reader. Enabled by the spirit, the diviner asks questions and creates patterns; the

[23] Musa Dube, "Divining Ruth for International Relations," in *Other Ways of Reading: African Women and the Bible,* ed. Musa Dube (Atlanta: Society of Biblical Literature, 2001), 179-195.

consulting reader must confirm or deny that the patterns represent what he/she knows about his/her life and relationships. He/she is charged with discerning and embracing what makes for the life of the community within which he/she also finds life. African Initiative Churches in Botswana use the Bible to diagnose the relationships of the consulting reader. Not all diviners are diviner-healers: the diviner-healer's goal is to "assess all existing social relations and [encourage] healthy relations."[24] For Dube, "the book [of Ruth], in other words, divines its readers, confirming or confronting their experiences and offering alternatives."[25] She then examines what the story tells us of the relationships of Israel and Moab, and what light this may throw on international relations. Here are some of her conclusions.

Ruth represents Moab, Naomi Judah; the relationships of the two are unhealthy. Judah is land of divine blessing, Moab land of divine absence, of famine, infertility and death. Married to a young man of Moab Ruth remained childless, but married to an old man in Judah she immediately had a child. Naomi answers Ruth's speech of belonging with silence. Dube agrees with Amy-Jill Levine[26] that Naomi does not commit herself to Ruth, and with Athalya Brenner[27] that Ruth's pledge to Naomi is not the mutual love of friends but akin to "a slave's love for his master in Exod 21:2-6." She clings to

---

[24] *Ibid.*, 184.

[25] *Ibid.*, 181.

[26]Carol A. Newsome and Sharon H. Ringe ,"Ruth," in *The Women's Bible Commentary,* ed.Carol A. Newsome and Sharon H. Ring (Louisville: Westminster John Knox, 1992), 80.

[27] Athalya Brenner, ed. *Ruth and Esther: A Feminist Companion to the Bible* (Sheffield: Sheffield Academic Press, 1999), 159.

Naomi only to become property bought and used to perpetuate the line of Mahlon—no relationship of equals. The son is born to Naomi, not to Ruth or both of them. "Ruth is acknowledged for serving the interests of Naomi/Judah." The reader is instructed to avoid Moab or embrace it at the cost of disaster and death. Judah refuses to recognize the divine powers at work in Moab. It is "unwilling to contribute equally to Moab. Judah rejects Moab's right to benefit equally from their relationship."[28] This is a paradigm of what is happening in our "globalized" world. But the health of our world calls for a "relationship of liberating interdependence." Dube concludes that

> creating and maintaining healthy relations is indispensable medication in healing our world, and in proclaiming life and success within and outside the nations.[29]

5. African Women's Hermeneutics

We see that African women use a variety of methods. Among members of the Circle, however, there are shared convictions.[30] The focus is on "doing theology from women's

---

[28] Dube, "Divining Ruth," 194.

[29] *Ibid.*, 194.

[30] In what follows, I rely mainly on the following: Musa Dube, "Introduction," in *Other Ways of Reading: African Women and the Bible*, ed. Musa Dube (Atlanta: Society of Biblical Literature; Geneva, Switzerland: World Council of Churches, 2001), 1-19; Mercy Amba Oduyoye, *Introducing African Women's Theology* (Cleveland: The Pilgrim Press; Sheffield: Sheffield Academic Press, 2001); Teresa Okure, "Feminist Interpretations in Africa," in *Searching the Scriptures: A Feminist Introduction*, ed. Elisabeth Schüssler Fiornza, (New York:

perspective."[31] American and European feminists focus on sex and gender, African American womanists and Latina *mujeristas* add concerns of race and class, while

> African women's hermeneutics embraces issues of sex, race, class and adds culture in a search for wholeness for the woman herself and for humanity.[32]

The quest is for the fullness of life, of men and women and of the cosmos itself. Teresa Okure of Nigeria asserts that what is at stake in women's struggle against patriarchy is nothing short of "humanity's own revolution."[33]

A double hermeneutics is advocated: biblical hermeneutics in dialogue with cultural hermeneutics.[34] No culture is perfect and the Bible contains unwelcome vestiges of ancient culture. Culture and Bible have been tools for the oppression and domination of women. Cultural hermeneutics critiques both and identifies elements that are life-affirming.[35] Biblical exegesis merges with theology in the one quest for "the full liberation of women and men in, by, and through

---

Crossroads, 1993), 76-85; idem, "Invitation to African Women's Hermeneutical Concerns," in *Interpreting the New Testament in Africa*, eds. Mary Getui, Tinyiko Maluleke, and Justin Ukpong (Nairobi: Acton Publishers, 2001), 42-67.

[31] Okure, "Invitation to African Women's Hermeneutical Concerns," 48.

[32] *Ibid.*, 49

[33] *Ibid.*, 42

[34] Oduyoye, *Introducing African Women's Theology*, 8.

[35] *Ibid.*, 11-14.

Christ."[36] These women "intertwine theology, ethics and spirituality ... [moving] to commitment, advocacy and a transforming praxis."[37] Historical theology (patristics, medieval dogmatics, the Reformation ...) is given no significant role.[38] Exegesis and theology start from reflection on stories from the Bible, Africa's history and culture and women's experiences of social change.[39] Dube employs

> storytelling as a feminist theory of analysis and as a method of rewriting the patriarchal silences about women's lives in the biblical texts and African history.[40]

African women read with the "sisterhood," which embraces Christians, Muslims, Hindus, and followers of African Traditional Religion. Sugirtharajah terms such reading "inter-faith hermeneutics."[41] While some accord authority to the Bible, for Dube and others authority belongs to what promotes life and wholeness for women and the community, no preference being given *prima facie* to the biblical canon. The Bible is read with the canons of African oral cultures and other religious canons.[42] Some invoke as canons the United Nations Declaration of Human Rights and the liberative Constitutions, like the new constitution of South Africa. The

---

[36] Okure, "Feminist Interpretations in Africa," 83.

[37] Oduyoye, *Introducing African Women's Theology*, 16.

[38] Oduyoye, *Introducing African Women's Theology*, 16.

[39] *Ibid.*

[40] Dube, "Introduction," *Other Ways of Reading*, 5.

[41] R. S. Sugirtharajah, "Inter-faith Hermeneutics: An Example and Some Implications," in *Voices from the Margin: Interpreting the Bible in the Third World*. Revised edition (Maryknoll: Orbis, 1995), 306-318.

[42] Dube, "Introduction," *Other Ways of Reading*, 14,

reader must never give up the task of discernment for what is life-giving and must read for healing, knowing that "all diviner-readers are not healer-diviners."[43]

[43] *Ibid.*, 17

WORKS CITED

Adamo, David Tuesday. "African Cultural Hermeneutics." In *Vernacular Hermeneutics*, ed. R. S. Sugirtharajah, 66-90. Sheffield, UK: Shefffield Academic Press, 1999.

Adeyemo, Tokunboh ed. *Africa Bible Commentary*. Nairobi, Kenya: WordAlive Publishers; Grand Rapids: Zondervan (By the ecumenical Association of Evangelicals of Africa [AEA]), 2006.

Amewowo, Wynnand. "Experiences and Discoveries with the Bible in West Africa." *Mission Studies* 3/1 (1986): 12-24.

Blount, Brian K. *Cultural Interpretation: Reorienting New Testament Criticism.* Minneapolis, MN: Fortress Press, 1995.

Brenner, Athalya. "Ruth as a Foreign Worker and the Politics of Exogamy." In *Ruth and Esther: A Feminist Companion to the Bible,* ed. Athalya Brenner, 158-162. Sheffield, UK: Sheffield Academic Press, 1999.

Des pretres noirs s'interrogent. Paris: Editions du Cerf, 1956.

Dickson, Kwesi and Paul Ellingworth, eds. *Biblical Revelation and African Beliefs.* London, UK: Lutherworth Press, 1969.

Dube, Musa. "Divining Ruth for International Relations." In *Other Ways of Reading: African Women and the Bible*, ed. Musa Dube, 179-195. Atlanta, GA: Society of Biblical Literature, 2001.

Dube, Musa, ed. *Other Ways of Reading: African Women and the Bible.* Atlanta: Society of Biblical Literature; Geneva, Switzerland: World Council of Churches, 2001.

Dube, Musa W. and Gerald O. West, eds. *The Bible in Africa: Transactions, Trajectories and Trends.* Leiden: E. J. Brill, 2000.

Ezeogu, Ernest. "Bible and Culture in African Christianity." *IRM* 87 (1998): 25-38.

Getui, Mary, Tinyiko Maluleke, and Justin Ukpong. "Bible Reading with a Community of Ordinary Readers." In *Interpreting the New Testament in Africa,* eds. Mary Getui, Tinyiko Maluleke and Justin Ukpong, 188-212. Nairobi, Kenya: Acton Publishers, 2001.

Kairos Document, *A Challenge to the Church: A Theological Comment on the Political Situation in South Africa.* 2nd edition. Grand Rapids, MI: Eerdmans, 1986.

Kanyoro, Musimbi R. A. "Biblical Hermeneutics: Ancient Palestine and the Contemporary World." *RevExp* 94 (1997): 363-378.

Levine, Amy-Jill. "Ruth." In *The Women's Bible Commentary*, eds. Carol A. Newsome and Sharon H. Ringe, 78-84. Louisville, KY: Westminster John Knox, 1992.

Masoga, Apheus. "Redefining Power: Reading the Bible in Africa from the Peripheral and Central Positions." In *Reading the Bible in the Global Village,* ed. Justin Ukpong, Musa Dube, Gerald West, et al., 95-109. Atlanta, GA: SBL, 2001.

Mugambi, Jesse. *From Liberation to Reconstruction: African Christian Theology after the Cold War.* Nairobi, Kenya: East African Educational Publishers, 1995.

Mugambi, Jesse. *Christian Theology and Social Reconstruction.* Nairobi, Kenya: Acton Publishers, 2003.

Oduyoye, Mercy Amba. *Introducing African Women's Theology.* Cleveland, OH: The Pilgrims Progress; Sheffield, UK: Sheffield Academic Press, 2001.

Okure, Teresa. "Feminist Interpretations in Africa." In *Searching the Scriptures: A Feminist Introduction,* ed. Elisabeth Schüssler Fiornza, 76-85. New York, NY: Crossroads, 1993.

Okure, Teresa. "Invitation to African Women's Hermeneutical Concerns." In *Interpreting the New Testament in Africa,* eds. Mary Getui, Tinyiko Maluleke, and Justin Ukpong, 42-67. Nairobi, Kenya: Acton Publishers, 2001.

Sugirtharajah, R. S. "Inter-faith Hermeneutics: An Example and Some Implications." In *Voices from the Margin: Interpreting the Bible in the Third World, revised edition,* ed. R.S. Sugirtharajah, 306-318. Maryknoll, New York: Orbis, 1995.

Tolbert, Mary Ann. "The Politics and Poetics of Location." In *Reading From This Place. Volume 1: Social Location and Biblical Interpretation in the United States,* eds. Fernando Segovia and Mary Ann Tolbert, 305-317. Minneapolis, MN: Fortress Press, 1995.

Ukpong, Justin. "Popular Readings of the Bible in Africa and Implications for Academic Readings." In *The Bible in Africa: Transactions, Trajectories and Trends,* eds. Gerald O. West and Musa W. Dube, 582-594. Leiden: E. J. Brill, 2001.

Ukpong, Justin. "Bible Reading with a Community of Ordinary Readers." In *Interpreting the New Testament in Africa,* eds. Mary Getui, Tinyiko Maluleke, and Justin Ukpong, 188-212. Nairobi, Kenya: Acton Publishers, 2001.

West, Gerald O. "Reading the Bible Differently: Giving Shape to the Discourses of the Dominated." *Semeia* 73 (1996): 21-41.

West, Gerald O. "Constructing Critical and Contextual Readings with Ordinary Readers," *Journal of Theology for South Africa* 92 (1997): 60-69.

Code Black: A Black Catholic Liberation Bioethics

Shawnee M. Daniels-Sykes, SSND
Mount Mary College

Based on a paper delivered during the 2008 Annual Meeting in Chicago, Daniels-Sykes, SSND proposes that the long history of neglect and abuse suffered by blacks at the hands of the health care industry results from entrenched assumptions fostered by Western philosophies and principles that guide mainstream medical ethics, particularly in light of the 1979 Belmont Report, produced in response to the infamous Tuskegee Syphilis Study. That the report failed to take into consideration the circumstances of poverty and race, factors key to our understanding those victimized by the Study, underscores the prevailing implicit assumptions of black inferiority. Daniels-Sykes, SSND advises that a black Catholic liberation bioethics must be developed, one that promotes a culture of life.

Worldwide hospital emergency codes are frequently denoted by a color: code red, code blue, code yellow, or code black. For each hospital the code color has a special denotation. A code red could mean a patient is having a heart attack and needs emergency attention; a code blue could refer to an emergency in the neonatal intensive care unit that needs a response; a code black could indicate massive casualty or other health threats experienced by black people that need to be addressed. No matter the code color when an emergency is announced a particular code team is summoned to come immediately to the rescue, to save a human life(s). This paper proposes that the history of racist medicine, the use of Western philosophic theories and principles that undergird mainstream bioethics, and black mistrust of the health care system and health care providers are primary reasons for the black health crisis in the USA that has an extensive history. In an August 2008 article, researchers from the Department of Medicine at the University of Minnesota acknowledge that:

> [o]ver the past two decades, a burgeoning literature has emerged that documents the deleterious effects of perceived discrimination on the health of racial and ethnic minorities, including poor mental health (e.g., depression, anxiety, psychological distress), poor physical health (e.g., cardiovascular disease, breast and prostate cancers), giving birth to preterm or low birth weight babies, and deleterious health behaviors such as smoking and alcohol use.[1]

As a result of this crisis, I believe that a 'code black' alarm needs to ring loudly, signifying the need to address and resolve the massive crisis in black health. The code calls forth lay health advocates to offer assistance to patients and clients

---

[1] Diana J. Burgess, Yingmei Ding, Margaret Hargroves, Michele van Ryan, Sean Phelan, "The Association between Perceived Discrimination and Underutilization of Needed Medical and Mental Health Care in a Multi-Ethnic Community Sample." *Journal of Health Care for the Poor and Underserved* 19 (August 2008): 895.

in order to relieve this crisis in black health. Creative and concrete ways are needed to liberate these ailing captives from: acute and chronic illnesses that might have been prevented, physical, social, and psychological disabilities that might have been prevented, and/or premature deaths that might also have been prevented, among others. The highly disproportionate rate of morbidity and mortality in the black community as compared to whites is the impetus for my idea of a Black Catholic liberation bioethics.

Black people hail from a culture of deep religious roots; they have found meaning in pain and suffering through the black spirituals and reflection of the paschal mystery of the Black Jesus. While acknowledging a mainstream secular approach to bioethics and highlighting a Black Catholic liberation bioethics, I discuss the black health crisis that persists, especially because a purely modern secular bioethical lens has been used to evaluate all ethical concerns in health care via the renowned *1979 Belmont Report.*[2] I maintain that in order for a black Catholic liberation bioethics to emerge that promotes a culture of life instead of a culture of death, the emphasis must be on black self-love, black self-esteem, black self-care, and black self-empowerment. A black Catholic liberation bioethics implies: a love for justice, active instead of passive-aggression, liberation, reconciliation, peacefulness, community, trust, honesty, authenticity, a listening heart, great communication skills, a tireless ability to negotiate the health

---

[2] The Belmont Report: Ethical Principles and Guidelines for the Protection of Human Subjects of Research (1979). See the National Institutes of Health website: http://ohsr.od.nih.gov/guidelines/belmont.html.

care system, as lay health advocates assist patients in responding proactively to significant health issues that stifle Black human flourishing. Constant are prayers and actions toward freedom from oppression, depression, anger, and anxiety. Of crucial importance is stopping the dysfunctional dance between white racism and black internalized oppression. Acknowledging that overt and covert racism persist are of great importance in addressing the black health crisis. Essential also is the vow not to be succumbed by this social evil. The onus is on members of the black community who must first move out of a victim stance or a finger pointing stance, to one that embraces black self-empowerment, black self-esteem, black self-care, and black self-love in order to cope directly with this enduring crisis in black health that is driven by our dance of racial oppression, fear, mistrust, and suspicion of the health care system and health care providers.

In this paper, I argue that the U.S. Government's promulgation of the July 1979 *Belmont Report*,[3] which includes ethical principles and guidelines for the protection of human subjects of research, ignores the long history of unethical medical treatment of black people in the American health care system and medical research institutions. The report, instead, contains four mid-level principles (i.e., respect for persons, beneficience, non-maleficience, and justice) which are derived from Western European philosophical

---

[3] Albert Jonsen, "On the Origins and Future of the Belmont Report," in *Belmont Revisited: Ethical Principles for Research with Human Subjects*, eds. James Childress, Eric M. Meslin, and Harold T. Shapiro (Washington, D.C.: Georgetown University Press, 2005), 3-12.

theories such as Immanuel Kant's deontology and categorical imperative, John Stuart Mill's utilitarianism, John Rawls' egalitarianism and social contractarianism, and Robert Nozick's libertarianism. Although no one single universal philosophical ethical theory could be deduced to create the four principles of bioethics, both the theories and principles play a huge role in the promotion of normative bioethics, or modern secular bioethics. These theories and principles are considered to be unbiased, impartial, universal, coherent and all-encompassing rather than focus on one's particular experience or social location. Essentially, they are considered good ethical theory and principles in the ethical decision-making process and are to be judiciously employed to safeguard human beings from physical and psychological harm in the research and/or clinical setting. I push for a black Catholic liberation bioethics as another approach to addressing the black health crisis and other bioethical concerns that continue to adversely affect black people.

To develop my argument, I propose: 1) to present an overview of the history of medical abuse of black people by members of US medical and research establishments; 2) to discuss the influence of the July 1979 *Belmont Report*, which is a direct response to the forty-year Tuskegee Syphilis Study on poor uneducated black men in Macon County Alabama, and finally; 3) to begin a discussion on what I am calling a black Catholic liberation bioethics as exemplified in a ministry of accompaniment that involves lay health advocates in relationship with patients/clients.

Overview of Blacks' Experiences in Health Care

Since the time of African chattel slavery, blacks have been the subject of research and medical abuse. According to bioethicist and journalist Harriet A. Washington, "[e]nslavement could not have existed and certainly could not have persisted without medical science. Physicians were very much dependent upon slaves, both for economic security and for the enslaved 'clinical material' that fed the American medical research and medical training that bolstered physicians' professional advancement."[4] The dialog *Dissecting Hall*, e.g., describes the way blacks were unwillingly and unwittingly dragged off for medical experimentation. Composed in the Antebellum Period, *Dissecting Hall* illustrates this notion about "clinical material," and refers very graphically to the blacks being kidnapped and cruelly used, through the removal of their organs and limbs, to satisfy scientific curiosity.[5] Blacks during the Antebellum Period had little control over medical decisions made to use their bodies or even to use their corpses

---

[4] Harriet A. Washington, *Medical Apartheid: The Dark History of Medical Experimentation on Black Americans From Colonial Times to the Present* (New York, New York: Doubleday Broadway Publishing Group, 2006), 26.

[5] This dialog was found in an article by Todd L. Savitt and is called "The Use of Blacks for Medical Experimentation and Demonstration in the Old South." *Journal of Southern History* 48 (August 1982): 341-2. In a footnote he gives credit to Anne Donato for the reference, which is preceded by this citation *Scribe* I (December 1951), 17. Unfortunately, I was not able to find the source to verify the conversation.

for medical research.[6] Medical personnel believed that blacks were different from whites and thus, inferior. From research on human bodies, for example, scientists documented that whites had the largest skulls, the largest brains, and were thus, the most intelligent with the best character of all the human beings.[7] To the contrary, Blacks had the smallest skulls, the smallest brains, and were thus, considered unintelligent with no character.[8]

During the eighteenth and nineteenth centuries, medical researchers continued to practice on blacks to develop their trade or clinical techniques. The Father of Surgical Gynecology, Dr. Marion Sims, for example, used African female slaves to perfect his vaginal-vesicular surgical procedure.[9] Sims repeatedly performed painful surgeries on twenty-six of these women who suffered from vaginal fistulas. His experimentation led to the development of a forerunner of the modern speculum. Moreover, experimentation with new treatment and drugs on slaves allowed Dr. Robert Jennings to be credited with the development of successful vaccination

---

[6] *Ibid.,* 331-48.

[7] Harriet A. Washington, *Medical Apartheid,* 35

[8] *Ibid.*, 35.

[9] LL Walls, "The Medical Ethics of Dr. J. Marion Sims: A Fresh Look at the Historical Record." *Journal of Medical Ethics* 32 (2006): 346-50; Leon R. Kapsalis, "Mastering the Female Pelvis: Race and the Tools of Reproduction," in *Skin Deep: Spirit Strong: The Black Female Body in American Culture,* ed. Kimberly Gisele Wallace-Sanders (Ann Arbor, Michigan: University of Michigan Press, 2002), 263-300.

against typhoid infection that resulted from his successful experimentation on thirty slaves and free blacks.[10]

Three twentieth century examples of medical experimental abuse and neglect toward blacks are as follows: The first concerns a 31-year-old black woman named Henrietta Lacks. In February 1951, when she walked through the doors of Johns Hopkins Hospital in Baltimore, Maryland bleeding profusely, she did not live to see that she would make Dr. George Gey famous only ten months after she died. Gey used Lacks' peculiar and highly potent cells to develop a medical specialty called a continuous cell-line, or HeLa cells.[11]

A second medical experimentation pertains to the United States Public Health Services Study, more popularly known as the Tuskegee Syphilis Study which lasted from 1932 to 1972. It involved 399 poor uneducated black men from Macon County Alabama. This government-sponsored experiment's main goal was to watch the progression of untreated syphilis in these men. It is important to note that another two hundred and one men comprised the control group. Whether in the experimental or control group, the human rights and dignity of

---

[10] Barbara L. Bernier, "Class, Race, and Poverty: Medical Technologies and Socio-Political Choices." *Harvard Blackletter Law Journal* 115 (1994): 119.

[11] W. Michael Byrd and Linda A. Clayton, *An American Health Dilemma: Race, Medicine, and Health Care in the United States: 1900-2000* (New York, New York: Routledge, 2002), 285-6.

these men were not only suppressed, but egregiously violated for forty years.

A third example refers to the 1960s and 1970s where illegal sterilizations were performed on black women without their informed consent and for no apparent medical reasons. "The violence was committed by doctors paid by the government to provide health care for these women. Teaching hospitals performed unnecessary hysterectomies on poor black women as practice for their medical residents."[12]

Important reasons for poor health for African Americans, more commonly referred to as the "slave health deficit" are deeply intertwined with and stem from the previous examples of racist medicine and other medically egregious acts against black people. For too many blacks, the knowledge of these medical experiments and many others not discussed in this essay leave an indelible mark of mistrust, fear, and suspicion towards the health care system and its health care providers. Although Title VI of the 1964 Civil Right Act sought to rectify the legacy of racist medicine, many blacks today continue to perceive racial discrimination and medical neglect by health care providers; they refuse to visit a provider to seek primary care, diagnostic screening, or lingering health concerns. Unfortunately, this Civil Rights Act left open too many opportunities for medical researchers and health care providers to continue to participate in unethical behaviors such

---

[12] Dorothy Roberts, *Killing the Black Body: Race, Reproduction, and the Meaning of Liberty* (New York, New York, Pantheon Books, 1997), 90.

as forced sterilizations on black women as noted above, unnecessary surgeries, medical experimentation, and inadequate health care.

More contemporarily, the 2003 Committee on Understanding and Eliminating Racial and Ethnic Disparities in Health Care, convened by the Institute of Medicine in Washington, D.C.,[13] unveiled and reported continual unethical behavior in health care that is connected with racial and ethnic bias and stereotyping. For example, in medical or clinical decision-making, even when patients are black and medically insured, some health care providers do not order the necessary diagnostic and screening tests to rule out a patient's chief complaint. Reportedly, some providers, "give an untreatable diagnosis to a patient, or order limited treatments, or deny radiation or chemotherapy for cancer, dialysis for kidney failure, and bypass or balloon surgery and a pacemaker for heart disease cases."[14] As a result of insufficient health care too many black people continue to become sicker and sicker. A code black alarm needs to ring loudly, signifying an emergency to save human lives, especially from preventable and curable diseases that lead to black peoples' highly disproportionate rates of morbidity and morality.

---

[13] See Institute of Medicine, *Unequal Treatment: Confronting Racial and Ethnic Disparities in Health Care* (Washington, D.C.: The National Academies Press, 2003), 102.

[14] Emilie M. Townes, *Breaking the Fine Rain of Death: African American Health Issues and a Womanist Ethic of Care* (New York, New York: Continuum Publishing Company, 1998), 117-8.

The January 2005 issue of *Morbidity and Mortality Weekly*, in particular, reveals that blacks continue to have highly disproportionate rates of medical and public health problems such as: various types of cancers, HIV/AIDS and other sexually transmitted infections, obesity, cardiovascular diseases, stokes, diabetes, hypertension, infant mortality, childhood asthma, unintentional accidents, homicides, and other health concerns. These serious health concerns may potentially lead to premature deaths, decreased quality of life, loss of economic opportunities, and ongoing mistrust of the health care system. Many black people might ponder this question: why trust physicians or medical researchers whom they perceive as violent, racist, non-caring, and abusive all because of their dark skin color, myths about their inferior mental status, and their Constitutional designation as 3/5th of a person?

A government-appointed commission comprised of philosophers, theologians, lawyers, physicians, nurses, etc. was charged with bringing some resolution to the human research and medical abuse, especially in light of the public disclosure of the Tuskegee Syphilis Study. It was thought that perhaps the commissioners' collaborative efforts to develop and implement the 1979 *Belmont Report*[15] would bring huge

---

[15] It is important to know that there were three primary documents that provide the foundation for efforts to protect human beings who participate in research: The *Nüremberg Code,* the *Declaration of Helsinki* and the *Belmont Report*. The *Nüremberg Code* is a statement on medical ethics that was issued in 1947 after the trial of 23 medical doctors accused of atrocities committed during the Nazi era in Europe in World War II. The *Declaration of Helsinki* on Ethical principle for Medical Research

resolutions and an end to the history of medical abuse and neglect. It is very unfortunate that this report does not address directly the health care system that is built on racist and egregious acts against black people. Instead the commissioners decided on a report that would focus on modern secular bioethics which is undergirded by Western European philosophical theories and four mid-level principles, both of which are intrinsic to an American liberal philosophy of justice. These theories and principles do not challenge institutionalized racism, white privilege, nor do they acknowledge the misuse and abuse of many black peoples' bodies for the development of American medicine and research.

The Influence of the 1979 *Belmont Report* on the Black Health Crisis

Public disclosure of the Tuskegee Syphilis Study prompted the need for government intervention to establish ethical principles and guidelines for the protection of human subject research. For example, on July 12, 1974, the National Research Act (Pub L. 93-348) was signed into law, which, in turn, established the National Commission for the Protection of Human Subjects of Biomedical and Behavioral Research. One of the responsibilities of the National Commission was to identify the basic ethical principles that should underline the conduct of biomedical and behavioral research involving

---

Involving Human Subjects was adopted by the World Medical Association (WMA) in its 18th General assembly in Helsinki, Finland in 1964. The *Belmont Report* is the one discussed in detail in this paper.

human subjects and to develop guidelines which should be followed to assure that such research is conducted in accordance with those principles.

After four years of deliberation, the commissioners published the *Belmont Report* which contained a detailed discussion of the four mid-level principles of bioethics: respect for person/autonomy, beneficience, non- maleficence, and justice.[16] They are mid-level principles because they were deduced from universal Western philosophical theories such as utilitarianism, Kantian deontology or the categorical imperative, egalitarianism, social contract theory, and libertarianism. The mid-level principles are believed "to be objective, rational, internally coherent, and consistent, universally applicable, detached from individual self-interest, and impersonal in their capacity to transcend the particularities of time and culture."[17] Extremely important to the *Belmont Report*, the four principles of bioethics are to be employed judiciously to prevent research and clinical practice abuses while treating everyone the same regardless of race, class, gender, creed, or national origin. The principles supposedly allow for a systematized way for prescriptive as opposed to descriptive judgments to be made in the ethical decision-making process.

---

[16] Albert Jonsen, "On the Origins and Future of the Belmont Report," 3-12.

[17] Daniel Callahan, "Universalism & Particularism: Fighting to a Draw." *The Hasting Center Report* 30 (January/February 2000): 40.

Often referred to as the principle of *autonomy*, respect for persons is the first principle of biomedical ethics. An autonomous individual is a free, independent, rational thinking, self-ruled individual who makes choices and decisions without external influence or force. Autonomy as it applies to research and the clinic process means that the free human person is the main focus of moral concern. Key to this principle is always the notion of a personal or individual freedom. To be autonomous requires that an individual understands correctly and clearly what is proposed. For example, in a research protocol or a clinical procedure after it is explained, one discerns whether or not to participate.[18]

Next, the principle of *beneficence* requires that human beings not only respect individual autonomy, but to do good (benevolence) by contributing to the well-being of persons.[19] Unlike the principle of respect for persons, this principle entails an obligation by the health care provider to protect persons from harm by maximizing anticipated benefits and minimizing possible risks of harm or burdens.

---

[18] Other words associated with autonomy include: individual choice, liberty rights, self-rule, freedom of the will, privacy, and self-government. Those who have diminished decisional capacity may need someone else to decide for them, which diminishes their autonomy. In this respect, these individuals are controlled by another's decisions, which Kant would claim is not autonomy but heteronomy.

[19] James Childress and Tom Beauchamp, *Principles of Bioethics*, (Washington, D.C.: Georgetown University, 1994), 259.

The principle of *non-maleficence* means that harm must not be caused intentionally. Although it has long roots that extend back to the Hippocratic Oath tradition and also is found in tenets of the Ten Commandments or the *Decalogue*,[20] it was a later addition to the initial three principles of bioethics. This principle has both secular and theological underpinnings. It is unethical to intentionally harm another.

Finally, the principle of *justice* defines what it means to treat others equitably or fairly. "The primary question raised with respect to the principle of justice is: who ought to receive the benefits of research and bear its burdens?"[21] This is a critically important question given the ethos of rugged individualism, white privilege, racism, capitalism, and the marginalization of the least fortunate, economically poor, or the working poor in our U.S. society.

In essence, the commissioners appeared to have established a win-win situation for patients/clients/research subjects alike in tandem with health care providers, or medical researchers. A main objective of the patient-physician relationship is that patient/client individual human rights are

---

[20] Here the *Decalogue* refers to Ten Commandments, or a series of ten laws found in the Book of Exodus (20:2-11) and Deuteronomy (5:6-15).

[21] See materials from the *Belmont Report 25th Anniversary Symposium and Webcast*, May 14, 2004, Medical College of Wisconsin. The event commemorates the 25th anniversary of the *Belmont Report* by reuniting key authors, staff, and the remaining members of the National Commission for the Protection of Human Subjects of Biomedical and Behavioral Research.

guaranteed, while the four principles of bioethics remain at the forefront of the relationship.

Theological ethicist Cheryl J. Sanders recognizes the major use of these aforementioned four principles especially as they are embedded into the fabric of our American ethos. For Sanders, "[o]ne of the most significant contributions thinkers of European and European-American descent have made to the field of bioethics is drawing on these ethical principles to make applications to a broad range of problems and cases."[22] However, Sanders critiques, "the apparent marginalization of race [in the development of these principles] indicates a devaluation of the [African American] community and belief systems characteristic of African American ethical discourse and social life."[23] Mindful that the *Belmont Report* was published seven years after the 1972 public disclosure of the Tuskegee Syphilis Study, its point of departure is not the socioeconomically poor and uneducated black men of this study, which speaks volumes about what normative bioethics is in USA society. Rather its point of departure includes principles based in a European and European-American ethos that tends to disregard the type of particularity that is characteristic of these socioeconomically poor and uneducated black men.

---

[22] Cheryl J. Sanders, "European-American Ethos and Principlism: An African-American Challenge," in *A Matter of Principles? Ferment in U.S. Bioethics,* ed. Edwin R. DuBose, Ronald P. Hamel, and Laurence J. O'Connell (Valley Forge, Pennsylvania: Trinity Press International, 1994), 148-63, esp. 148.

[23] *Ibid.,* 148.

The principles are to be applied universally and presumed to be cross-culturally inclusive in secular moral ethics. Sanders declares that these principles tend to be "dualistic, exclusive, individualistic, secular, atheistic, inflexible, materialistic and harbor the necessary and sufficient conditions for the propagation of racism."[24] Bioethicist Annette Dula echos Sanders' critique. She further notes that "inattention to cultural and societal aspects of health care may be attributed in part to the mainstream Western philosophical theories and principles. Furthermore, these theories and principles presented primarily as a thinking enterprise in bioethics are rarely used to advocate for change, social justice, or societal transformation.[25]

Hence, by ignoring the relevant features of the men who participated in the Tuskegee Syphilis Study, arguably, the commissioners charged with the development of the *Belmont Report* failed to protect *all* human subjects in a holistic manner. The vulnerable research subjects of the Tuskegee Syphilis Study were deceived and coerced into participating in the forty-year study that investigated the progression of syphilis. Because of their race and socioeconomic status, United States Public Health Services researchers preyed on these men's presumed intellectual inferiority and

---

[24] Cheryl J. Sanders, "European-Americans and Principlism," 151.

[25] Annette Dula, "Toward an African-American Perspective on Bioethics," *Cross Cultural Perspectives in Medical Ethics, 2nd Edition*, ed. Robert M. Veatch (Sudbury, Massachusetts: Jones and Bartlett Publishers, 2000), 357-69, esp. 360.

economically impoverished state and therefore, saw no need to include in the research protocol ways to seek a deeper understanding of the social, economic, and political experiences that shaped their life's history. These poor black men were deemed expendable and were used and abused for the researchers' professional development and self-aggrandizement.

According to physician and bioethicist Edmund D. Pelligrino in order

> [t]o understand the moment and direction of moral decisions in any person's life, we need as much knowledge as possible of the internal and external forces that have shaped that person's life's history. A clinical case history or a moral dilemma is always part of a larger life story, an act or a scene in the complex drama of life.[26]

For example, the African American ethos, which is largely derived from traditional African cultures, is essentially holistic, inclusive, communalistic, spiritual, theistic, improvisational, and humanistic in many ways that the European-American ethos is not."[27] The commissioners' use of the impartial, universal, secular, and so-called all-encompassing principles allowed them to miss a full-blown discussion on how white racism works in the medical abuse

---

[26] Edmund D. Pelligrino, "Bioethics at Century's Turn: Can Normative Ethics be Retrieved?" *Journal of Medicine and Philosophy* 25 (2000): 664.

[27] *Ibid.*, 151.

and maltreatment of these men. Instead they embraced the 'normativity of whiteness'[28] in the mere employment of these four principles.

Philosopher Cornel West writes of this concern also, while challenging white philosophers to face up to the historic and current implications of mainly focusing in on the works of white thinkers.[29] He observes that these [Western European philosophies] were used strategically to "promote black inferiority and constituted the European background which suppressed black diasporan struggles for identity, dignity (self-confidence, self-respect, self-esteem)."[30] Furthermore, bioethicist and anthropologist Catherine Myser notes that the use of these universal philosophies fosters a lack of attention to difference (i.e., of the research participants) and promotes white supremacist privilege,[31] reflective of the Tuskegee Syphilis Study's principle investigators from the United States Public Health Department. One must ask if employing these

---

[28] Catherine Myser, "Difference from Somewhere: The Normativity of Whiteness in Bioethics in the United States." *American Journal of Bioethics* 3 (2003): 1-11.

[29] Cornel West, "Race and Modernity," in *The Cornel West Reader* (New York, New York: Basic *Civitas* Books, 1999), 55-86.

[30] Cornel West, "The New Cultural Politics of Difference," in *The Cornel West Reader* (New York, New York: Basic *Civitas* Books, 1999), 119-39, esp. 128.

[31] Catherine Myser, "Difference from Somewhere: The Normativity of Whiteness in Bioethics in the United States." *American Journal of Bioethics* 3 (2003): 1.

principles has something to do with continuing racist medicine and many blacks' perceived racial discrimination. Is there a link between the theories and principles to the persistent black health crisis in the United States? When is a 'code black' going to sound to address the black health crisis that is undergirded by a racist medicine, and the long history of black exploitation and abuse in medical research and the clinical setting?

Since the *Belmont Report* seemingly did nothing directly to address the particular social location of the black research participants of the Tuskegee Syphilis Study, arguably, one can make the case that this infamous study remains linked to many of blacks' deep-seated attitudes of distrust, suspicion, and fear of health care providers and medical institutions in the United States.[32] This is despite the fact that medical facilities and health care providers are regulated by local and federal governmental standards and codes of ethics. Today "the federal government has been shown more likely to close down entire university research programs under the aegis of the Federal Drug Administration (FDA) when embarrassed by federally sponsored abuse."[33] All standards and codes were created to ensure human protection from any medical abuse—

[32] Peter A. Clark, "Prejudice and the Medical Profession: Racism, Sometimes Overt, Sometimes Subtle, Continues to Plague U.S. Health Care." *Health Progress* 84 (September 2003): 12-23.

[33] Harriet A. Washington, *Medical Apartheid,* 388.

research, academic, and/or clinical.[34] For the standards and codes, the individual patient or client is of most importance; they must be protected from medical harm. Individuals have the right to make informed decisions or give informed consent to undergo health care screenings, diagnosis, and/or treatments.

Still too many blacks remain afraid, carry negative attitudes, and are reluctant to engage the health care system. Too many perceive racial discrimination by health care providers and do not want to be bothered with them. Their dispositions lead to reasons for the high rates of black morbidity and mortality. Indeed a need exists for black people to move from so much paralyzing fear, anger, suspicion, and mistrust of health care providers in the health care system to a greater ability to engage in self-care, self-love, to have high self-esteem, and to be self-empowered persons. Today a need exists for health care providers and medical researchers to acknowledge the horrible history of black medical abuse and neglect, but a need also exists for black people to regain trust in the health care system that, for the most part, is very responsive to the code black alarm.

I offer that the Catholic Church in black communities, especially, has a major role to play in helping to liberate the ailing captives by focusing on health promotion and primary prevention. What does a black Catholic liberation bioethics

---

[34] J. Wasserman, M.A. Flannery, and J.M. Clair, "Raising the Ivory Tower: The Production of Knowledge and Distrust of Medicine among African Americans." *Journal of Medical Ethics* 33 (2007):177-80.

have to offer in addressing the black health crisis in this country? What does a black Catholic liberation bioethics have to offer to shore up the deficiencies of principles derived from Western European philosophical thought?

A Black Catholic Liberation Bioethics

I am defining a Black Catholic liberation bioethics as it not only transcends or moves beyond mainstream secular bioethical theories and principles but it means that Christians must do the will of God as modeled in the liberating Gospel of Jesus Christ. That will is in the context of communal relationships (or as I will later discuss, lay health advocates) that seek the realization of the wholeness of life despite egregious unethical acts done unto black bodies and black lives in clinical medicine and scientific research. "That wholeness of life embraces the total existence of human life in the past; it embraces the total meaning of black *being* with regard to the past, present, and future."[35] A black Catholic liberation bioethics is also reconciling and liberating. Reconciliation and liberation [36] underscore hope for healing

---

[35] Allan Aubrey Boesak, *Farewell to Innocence: A Socio-Ethical Study on Black Theology and Black Power* (Maryknoll, New York: Orbis Books, 1977), 141.

[36] Dwight Hopkins, *Introducing Black Theology of Liberation* (Maryknoll, New York, Orbis Books, 1999), 62-3. It is important to note that, traditionally, within the black political theology trend, Cone will come to reconciliation after a redistribution of white political power. Roberts, in contrast, stands for black liberation against white racism and, simultaneously, for genuine reconciliation with white people. He targets liberation and reconciliation as the "twin goals" and "two main poles" of

and freedom of black people from the memory and experience of egregious unethical medical acts. One method of critically examining the wholeness of black human life in tandem with reconciliation and liberation is through the pastoral circle.

The pastoral circle is a three-part social analytical process, including: *seeing, judging,* and *acting.* I am adding the need for *understanding* between seeing and judging in this circle, lest we prejudge too quickly, starting to analyze and make decisions about the situation only after we see. In the acting part, I propose the notion of a ministry of accompaniment for black patients/clients via the use of lay health advocates.

The pastoral circle allows one to *see* that clinical medicine and scientific research in the United States has not been the most respectful of black bodies or black lives. The memory of it persists today and is manifested in fear and mistrust of the health care system. As aforementioned, health statistics reveal that blacks continue to be adversely affected

---

black theology. Liberation calls for black people's freedom from the bondage of white racism. And reconciliation suggests that black freedom does not deny white humanity but meets whiteness on equal ground. Roberts seeks to develop both goals in a balanced way: that is, in terms of (1) always explaining one in relation to the other, and (2) using them as the core ground which he weaves his systematic theology. I am using these terms: Reconciliation and Liberation in the context of bioethics—healing and freedom of black people from the memory and experience of egregious unethical acts. It takes two to continue to dance of the oppressor and oppressed relationship and both need to be reconciled and liberated to stop the continuous dysfunctional dance.

by the slave health deficit or black health crisis. Empirical data on health reveals that overall black people experience highly disproportionate rates of preventable and treatable diseases such as diabetes, hypertension, stroke, breast and prostate cancer, mental illness, problems from illegal drug use and alcoholism, HIV/AIDS and STI's, among others. Electively induced abortions and homicides occur at a disproportionately high rate too. A huge ethical issue for anyone concerned is that the black population rate is not growing consistently, rapidly, and exponentially upward as other U.S. populations are. Aware of this data, one must not find it difficult to ponder and to ask, are black people in danger of extinction or how close is it to the full extermination of this population? What must be done to increase the population growth rate in this group?

Before moving on to judging the empirical data, one must *understand* that despite abuse, exploitation, and mistreatment, for centuries, black people 'got over,' making a way out of no way through faith in the Jesus Christ, the Liberator. For theologian J. Deotis Roberts this is because

> [O]urs has been a hope against hope. Indeed, for us, faith has been the substance of things hoped for. It has been based upon unseen evidence…The black faithful knows what it means to reach out into the darkness and grasp the hand of God, to take a step at a time in the shadows and to find

> such trust better than light, better than a well-trodden path.[37]

They understand that deep down inside that God did not make junk; that God created everyone and everything good not to be used and abused by another.

A *judgment* can be made on the three broadly construed aforementioned accounts: first, members of the national commission who developed the 1979 *Belmont Report* missed a great opportunity to recall the long history of medical abuse and maltreatment in the black population, and to delineate a plan that addressed how to eradicate or dismantle racism instantly in the health care and medical research system. Secondly, black people continue to perceive racial discrimination in the health care provider and patient/client relationship despite professional ethical codes and standards, patients' bill of rights, the process of informed consent, the four principles of bioethics, etc. Various types of professional journal articles and books report that still many black people do not receive the same kind of medical treatment as their white counterparts even when black people have the appropriate medical insurance. This information does not assist in remedying black people's perceived racial discrimination. Rather, this perception seems to be perpetuated consciously or unconsciously by them with no clear end in sight. Thirdly, many black people today lack the financial, mental, and/or physical ability to engage in primary

---

[37] J. Deotis Roberts, *A Black Political Theology* (Louisville, Kentucky: John Knox Press, 1974), 64.

prevention and health promotion. They hold onto deeply embedded fear, mistrust, and suspicion of the health care system and their providers. Many are unemployed or underemployed and, therefore, lack adequate health insurance or are completely uninsured. These three accounts require actions that significantly decrease the health crisis in black communities across the United States. Again, a *code black alarm* needs to be called, generating *a black Catholic liberation bioethics*.

A concrete *action* that I offer in putting into practice a black Catholic liberation bioethics is to train lay health advocates who are attentive, intelligent, rational, and responsible about this emergency in black health. Characteristically, lay health advocates must strongly desire to assist in finding a resolution to the problems and barriers to black health care in tandem with championing primary care prevention and health promotion. This idea of lay health advocates comes from my thinking about the notion of medical foster parents for children, although there are many differences. Medical foster parents, for example, assist critically ill children because the parents for whatever reasons are not able to follow through with the necessary and demanding medical regiment that the child needs in order to improve or recover from his/her illness. Medical foster parents work closely with the biological parents and child to get the child's health needs addressed adequately and in a timely manner.

Nevertheless, lay health advocates must feel a deep sense of urgency while they respond to a code black, and/or while promoting a culture of life. Through an intensive formation process they are trained to come to the rescue. Acknowledging the time and dedication needed for this ministry training and formation, their ministry as lay health advocates is to offer a peaceful, pastoral, and prayerful presence as they accompany the patient/client in his/her health care situation. These advocates understand what it means to be a part of a sacred trust because "to be a Christian is to live as part of a body and the parts need always to be developing their relationships with one another."[38]

Ultimately, they become very adept at journeying in a mutual and respectful way with the patient/client: in communicating with the medical professionals, in negotiating bureaucratic health insurance companies, in following up with medical concerns or referrals, in helping to discuss and to organize prescription medications, among many other areas. In addition, lay health advocates are not afraid to explore further options for health care with the patient/client, or assist in obtaining second opinions with the patient/client. In essence, they embrace and live out the words of the Lukan Jesus in Luke 4: 18-19:

> "The spirit of the Lord is upon me, because he has chosen me to bring good news to the poor. He has sent me to proclaim liberty to the captives and recovery of sight to the blind, to set free the

---

[38] Barbara J. Blodgett, *Lives Entrusted: An Ethic of Trust for Ministry* (Minneapolis, MN: Fortress Press, 2008), 1.

> oppressed and announce that the time has come when the Lord will save his people."

Ultimately, the goal of the lay health advocate and the patients/clients is to respond to the code black alarm so as to help in the realization of a black Catholic liberation bioethics through a ministry of accompaniment.

Summary and Conclusion

In this paper, I attempted to look at the crisis in black health that has a long history extending back to the Antebellum Period. The public disclosure of the forty-year Tuskegee Syphilis Study provoked the United States Government to appoint a national commission to establish ethical guidelines for research on human subjects contained in the *1979 Belmont Report*. These guidelines include the four principles of bioethics that were derived from Western European philosophies or normative ethical theories. In a close examination of this ethical system in which mainstream bioethics is built, I critiqued the fact that these ethical theories and principles promote what Catherine Myser 'a lack of attention to difference.' Further, historically, Western European philosophies were used strategically to promote black inferiority and constituted the European background which suppressed black diasporan struggles for identity and dignity (self-confidence, self-respect, and self-esteem). I argued that the use of these philosophies and principles ignore the long history of unethical medical treatment of black people in the American health care system and medical research institutions. The commissioners missed an opportunity to acknowledge that American health care is a racist institution. An emergency black health crisis continues today and that the onus is on members of black communities and others of good will to respond creatively and concretely to address the dire health problems facing this population. I stressed that a code black alarm has been ringing loudly for years, indeed centuries and that people need to come to the rescue immediately before the black population vanishes. I suggest that the emergency black health crisis can be addressed through a ministry of accompaniment program that includes lay health advocates who are sold on the idea of a black Catholic liberation bioethics. Through extensive training and formation they make a formal commitment to journey mutually, responsibly, and respectfully with patients and clients who need assistance navigating the complex health care system, and in helping them to understand the need for health promotion and primary care prevention. In essence, these lay health advocates are trained to respond to the code black alarm, in light of a black Catholic liberation bioethics.

WORKS CITED

Bernier, Barbara L. "Class, Race, and Poverty: Medical Technologies and Socio-Political Choices." *Harvard Blackletter Law Journal* 115 (1994):115-43.

Blodgett, Barbara J. *Lives Entrusted: An Ethic of Trust for Ministry.* Minneapolis, MN: Fortress Press, 2008.

Boesak, Allan Aubrey. *Farewell to Innocence: A Socio-Ethical Study on Black Theology and Black Power.* Maryknoll, New York: Orbis Books, 1977.

Burgess, Diana J., Yingmei Ding, Margaret Hargroves, Michele van Ryan, Sean Phelan." The Association between Discrimination and Underutilization of Needed Medical and Mental Health Care in a Multi-Ethnic Community Sample." *Journal of Health Care for the Poor and Underserved* 19 (August 2008): 894-911.

Byrd, W. Michael and Linda A. Clayton. *An American Health Dilemma: Race, Medicine, and Health Care in the United States: 1900-2000.* New York, New York: Routledge, 2002.

Callahan, Daniel. "Universalism & Particularism: Fighting to a Draw." *The Hasting Center Report* (January/February 2000): 37-44.

Childress, James and Tom Beauchamp. *Principles of Bioethics.* Washington, D.C.: Georgetown University Press, 1994.

Clark, Peter A. "Prejudice and the Medical Profession: Racism, Sometime Overt, Sometimes Subtle, Continue to Plague U.S. Health Care." *Health Progress* 84 (September 2003): 12-23.

Dula, Annette. "Toward an African-American Perspective on Bioethics." In *Cross Cultural Perspectives in Medical Ethics 2nd edition*, ed. Robert M. Veatch, 357-69. Seabury, Massachusetts: Jones and Bartlett Publishers, 2000.

Hopkins, Dwight. *Introducing Black Theology of Liberation.* Maryknoll, New York: Orbis Books, 1999.

Institute of Medicine. *Unequal Treatment: Confronting Racial and Ethnic Disparities in Health Care.* Washington, D.C.: The National Academies Press, 2003.

Jonsen, Albert. "On the Future of the Belmont Report." In *Belmont Revisited: Ethical Principles for Research with Human Subjects,* eds. James Childress, Eric M. Meslin and Harold T. Shapiro, 3-12. Washington, D.C.: Georgetown University Press, 2005.

Kapsalis, Leon R. "Mastering the Female Pelvis: Race and the Tools of Reproduction." In *Skin Deep: Spirit Strong: The Black Female Body in American Culture,* ed. Kimberly Gisele Wallace-Sanders, 263-300. Ann Arbor, Michigan: University of Michigan Press, 2002.

Myser, Catherine. "Difference from Somewhere: The Normativity of Whiteness in Bioethics in the United States." *American Journal of Bioethics* 3 (2003): 1-11.

Pelligrino, Edmund. D. "Bioethics at Century's Turn: Can Normative Ethics Be Retrieved." *Journal of Medicine and Philosophy* 25 (2000): 655-75.

Roberts, Dorothy. *Killing the Black Body: Race, Reproduction, and the Meaning of Liberty.* New York, New York: Pantheon Books, 1997.

Roberts, J. Deotis. *A Black Political Theology.* Louisville, Kentucky: John Knox Press, 1974.

Sanders, Cheryl J. "European-American Ethos and Principlism: An African American Challenge." In *A Matter of Principles? Ferment in U.S. Bioethics,* ed. Edwin R. DuBose, Ronald P. Hamel, and Laurence J. O'Connell, 148-53. Valley Forge, Pennsylvania: Trinity Press International, 1994.

Savitt, Todd L. "The Use of Blacks for Medical Experimentation and Demonstration in the Old South." *Journal of Southern History* 48 (August 1982): 331-48.

Townes, Emilie M. *Breaking the Fine Rain of Death: African American health Issues and a Womanist Ethic of Care.* New York, New York: Continuum Publishing Company, 1998.

Walls, LL. "The Medical Ethics of Dr. J. Marion Sims: A Fresh Look at the Historical Record." *Journal of Medical Ethics* 32 (June 2006):346-50.

Washington, Harriet A. *Medical Apartheid: The Dark History of Medical Experimentation on Black Americans from Colonial Times to the Present.* New York, New York: Doubleday Broadway Publishing Group, 2006.

Wasserman, J., M. A. Flannery, and J. M. Clair. "Raising the Ivory Tower: The Production of Knowledge and Distrust of Medicine among African Americans." *Journal of Medical Ethics* 33 (2007): 177-80.

West, Cornel. "Race and Modernity." In *The Cornel West Reader,* ed. Cornel West, 55-86. New York, New York: Basic Civitas Books, 1999.

The Flames of Namugongo: Issues Around Theological Narrativity, Heteronormativity, Globalization, and AIDS in Africa

Ken Hamilton, SVD
University of Notre Dame de Namur

Hamilton's paper, delivered during the 2008 Annual Meeting in Chicago, uses the hagiography of Charles Lwanga and the Martyrs of Uganda to reveal an unrelenting problem of the Church – the ways in which the assumptions of heternormativity and sodomitical discourse drown out the voices of those who do not fall into heteronormative sexual and/or gendered identities, and lead to the open persecution, imprisonment, and torture of gay, lesbian, bisexual, and transgendered persons in Uganda, and in fact all over Africa. Casting those with 'othered' sexual identities as evil, or even simply turning a deaf ear to the persecution faced by those persons, has both explicitly and implicitly added to their suffering, including ignoring the plight of AIDS victims. The solution may lie in our efforts to understand the deities of Africa.

> Historically, the European construction of sexuality coincides with the epoch of imperialism and the two inter-connect.
>
> ~~ Kobena Mercer and Isaac Julien[1]

A. The Story: Opening Scene

The Passion of the Uganda Martyrs begins as the young male royal pages, assembled outside the Kabaka's (the Bugandan king's) ivory court, are about to process into African Christianity's most celebrated martyr-passion narrative. The year is 1886, four years before the British annexation of Uganda. The leader of the pages, a certain Charles Lwanga, turns to the others and says "in a firm voice, 'let us go in.'"[2] The Roman Catholic priest John F. Faupel writes the following, in the most authoritative and thorough recounting of the martyrdom to date, *African Holocaust: The Story of the Uganda Martyrs*:

> Followed by the pages, Lwanga went through the gateway to the ivory court… Their passage… accompanied by taunts and cries of derision from the hundred or so executioners already gathered there. When the last of the pages had greeted him,

---

[1]Rudi C. Bleys, *The Geography of Perversion: Male-to-Male Sexual Behavior Outside the West and the Ethnographic Imagination, 1750-1918* (New York: New York University Press, 1995), 1.

[2]J. F. Faupel, *African Holocaust: The Story of the Uganda Martyrs*. (New York: P. J. Kenedy and Sons, 1962), 149. Unless otherwise noted, my references to Faupel are to his 1962 edition. The only difference in the texts, including pagination, is that the 1965 edition includes a short appendix with excerpts from the sermon of Paul VI at the 1964 canonization.

> (Kabaka) Mwanga asked, "Are they all here?" Being assured that none [were] missing, he ordered the gates to be closed and then, pointing towards the reed fence to his left, said, "Now, let everyone who follows the religion of the white men go over there...Those who are not Christian must remain near me."[3]

At once, Charles Lwanga stood up, saying as he did so: "That of which a man is fully conscious he cannot disavow." Then taking Kizito (the youngest) by the hand, and closely followed by the other Christian pages, he walked calmly to the spot indicated by the Kabaka.[4] Then began the long march to the hill of execution: Namugongo Hill.

A description of execution day—June 3rd, 1886 (Ascension Day) —reads like a classic Christian martyr-passion, having many of the genre's classic characters and scenes: innocent youths passionate in their new faith; a fateful confrontation with a demonized ruler; the refusal to "apostatize" or escape death, torment and torture; visions of Christ; pious affirmations and last words; encounters with witnesses along the way to execution; stripping of clothes; final exhortations and calling out to God; execution; and finally, the stories of the witnesses afterwards. Faupel's version—his telling—continues to evoke the macabre and the surreal. In fact, the very graphic scenes included castrations, dismemberments and, of course, the burnings.

---

[3]Ibid., 149-150.
[4]Ibid., 150.

Cultural theorist Rudi Bleys gives us a painful look at the spark that set off not only this martyrdom but the civil war that lead to the colonial state now known as Uganda. That "spark" is the refusal of the royal pages to have sexual relationships with the king: Mwanga II.

> Mwanga, the leader of the [Ganda people] from 1884-1897 […] maintained a "harem" full of pageboys and resisted Christianization as it became clear that anal intercourse had to be renounced. As gradually more and more boys, who had converted to either Protestantism or Catholicism, refused sexual services to Mwanga and his entourage, a conflict arose. When his favourite pageboy, Mwafu, resisted as well, Mwanga went into a paroxysm of rage and several boys were killed. It is said that about one hundred boys, later turned into the Martyrs of Buganda, had died.[5]

The framing or telling of this story as a high tale—a Manichean confrontation of good and evil with the former being virgin pages who were martyred for their "faith" —is, indeed, a "Faith" that stands on a battleground between hetero and other-than-hetero desire and behavior. The "evil" character in this tale is a king who, because he is framed as such (and also because he is remembered over and over again in this telling), is basically diluted to "predator," even

---

[5]Rudi C. Bleys, *The Geography of Perversion: Male-to-Male Sexual Behavior Outside the West and the Ethnographic Imagination, 1750-1918* (New York: New York University Press, 1995), 172.

"pedophile."[6] This gives the story both a mythic and a scandalous overtone. On one level, this story, when sublimated, courteously told, brushed over with high theology, or with all the gruesome details deleted, can be proclaimed in the highest of hagiographical language, placed on calendars, and even celebrated at high liturgy. On the level of "scandal," however, it must be whispered and shushed, making it more powerful as an "open secret."

The Uganda martyr story, moreover, is a "colonial hagiography," one written at the cusp of colonization. It is a colonial hagiography because it "colonizes," both the geographies of mind and (earthly) territory. It is one of several very successful saint stories, Blessed Kateri Tekawitha of the Mohawks being another. Her story has been called a "hagiographical *tour de force*," because it was used to convince Europeans—filled with fears of race mixing and the conviction that chastity and Indian women were contradictions in terms—that, in fact, these were not contradictions.[7] The same is true of the story of Charles Lwanga and his Companions. For it too had to reconcile seemingly

---

[6]This is not Faupel's doing; nor is it just the telling of the original framers, such as Fr. J. P. Thoonen who wrote the original *Black Martyrs*. But these original accounts of the story have been overwritten by the anti-homosexual language, the abomination speech, of a very loud rightist contingent; from thus has arisen the charge of "pedophile."

[7] Her life narrative was originally composed by Jesuit Pierre Cholenc at Montreal, published in Paris in 1717, and translated by another Jesuit, Juan de Urtassum in 1724. It was "an unusual instance of a text" circulating through the Catholic Atlantic world, then from the northern empire of France, via Europe, to the southern empire of Spain (Greer and Bilinkoff, 2003, 236, xix).

irreconcilable objects for the European Catholic: "Africa" and "pure saintly boys." Lwanga and his companions are now constructed as African Dominic Savios—an Italian boy renowned for his "priceless innocence"; this truly makes their story another hagiographical *tour de force*.[8] Like Tekawitha, the Ugandan pages serve as templates of purity and asceticism familiar to the European.

B. The Issue of Heterosexism

When I finished delivering this title at a Black Catholic Theological Symposium, an African colleague commented, quite straightforwardly, that "homosexuality is considered an abomination in Africa." My immediate read of what he was saying was something very blunt and to the point: "Keep your arrogance off Africa. Keep your western neocolonialism and decadence off us. She has enough problems as it is without being connected to your AIDS-causing 'homosexual agenda' and its white privileged gay tourists and predators." Fine, perhaps I put too much into a single comment from one individual, but such a critique is out there! And even we who are members of the African Diaspora had best be careful of falling into the often racist observations about Africa of the "Gay International." For Joseph Massad, this phenomenon describes the missionary mentality of so many Western organizations and scholars regarding non-Western "gender variant" (etc.) populations. It is these missionary tasks, the discourse that produces them, and the organizations that

---

[8] Donald L. Boisvert, *Sanctity and Male Desire: A Gay Reading of Saints* (Cleveland: Pilgrim Press, 2004), 127.

represent them which constitute what I will call the Gay International.[9]

I acknowledge my colleague's critique, with all its harshness, bitterness, and truth. Indeed, I would add my own curses. I would see many reasons to leave Africa out of any queer analysis whatsoever because of what South African cultural theorist Neville Hoad points out as its radical alterity.[10] That is, even the best in the west—like our beloved Audre Lorde—often fall short of truly understanding what they see when they see "Africa."[11]

But this essay is not about discovering or describing some African "queerness"; nor is my focus on constructions such as "homosexuality" or "Africa" *per se*. This essay, in other words, is not anthropological. It is essentially about the nature of the discourses—theological, ethical, political, global—going on right now over the subject of homosexuality and Africa. It is about what I have seen and heard and researched regarding homophobic condemnations of same-sex behavior

---

[9]Joseph A. Massad. "Re-Orienting Desire: The Gay International and the Arab World," in *Desiring Arabs*, ed. Joseph Massad (Chicago: University of Chicago Press, 2008), 161.

[10]Neville Hoad, *African Intimacies: Race, Homosexuality, and Globalization* (Minneapolis: University of Minnesota Press, 2007). That is, that analysis that interrupts the assumptions of heterosexism.

[11]Ibid., xxiv-xxv. Hoad was referring to some stereotypes Lorde may have invoked in *Sister Outsider* (Trumansberg, N.Y.: The Crossing Press, Feminist Series, 1984). Hoad, moreover, wonders if anti-homosexuality on the part of Africans is not itself a "displaced resistance to perceived and real encroachments on neo-colonial national sovereignty by economic and cultural globalization. Op cit, xii-xiii.

and the effect that may have on the spread of AIDS. Therefore, the problem of heterosexism and its effects, its serious effects, must be discussed. By heterosexism I mean the "infallible" regimes of truth that dictate that all things—and the sacred "norms" that guide them—are, should be, and must be ruled by the "natural" and organizing principle of reproduction. It includes the criminalization of non-hetero behavior and the systematic, institutionalized, routine, and pervasive exclusion of any truth outside the heteronorm.[12] As a man of the Christian church, whose mission has been tainted with racism, imperialism, sexism, and homophobia, I have some obligation to raise my voice and address these issues for Africa and the world, particularly for my own Afri-diasporic community. So the first thing I said in response to my African colleague's warning that "homosexuality is considered an abomination in most of Africa." is "Yes, that's exactly my point!" "Abomination," in fact, is a word taken right from the scriptures, particularly in Leviticus 18:22. It, therefore, was placed onto the lips of Africans by missionaries, thus reinforcing my agreement with progressive ethicists like Daniel C. Maguire, who says in his introduction to the anthology *Heterosexism in Contemporary World Religion*, "Heterosexism, Not Homosexuality is the Problem[!]"[13]

---

[12]Heterosexism actually harms heterosexuals too in that it does not allow for any mature examination of the full range of their desires and excludes from society the creative contributions of their non-hetero neighbors.

[13]Daniel C. Maguire, "Heterosexism, Not Homosexuality is the Problem," in *Heterosexism in Contemporary World Religion: Problem and Prospect*, ed. Marvin Ellison and Judith Plaskow (Cleveland: Pilgrim Press, 2007), 1.

> Homosexuality is not a problem: heterosexism is a problem, and not just for sexual minorities. To think of homosexuality as a “problem”—which even persons of liberal bent can do—is a distraction and a surrender to the unjust and poisonous prejudice of heterosexism.
> Homophobia has, in irony, been called “the last respectable prejudice,”
> ...Unlike its cousins anti-Semitism, sexism, and racism, heterosexism has enjoyed undue immunity from critique, especially religious critique. Worse yet, religions have been the major offenders in fomenting prejudice against sexual minorities.[14]

That is to say, if homosexuality is a “western import”—as it is often tagged—then so is homophobia and heterosexism. And if homosexuality is viewed throughout Africa as an “abomination” —and, indeed, if this attitude hinders in any way a proper approach to AIDS, in terms of treatment, understanding how HIV is spread, dissemination of effective safeguards, etc.—then, truly, homophobia is the problem!

The title of my paper is drawn from my dissertation in which I addressed the ways Christian theology, ethics, hagiography/martyrology, and sexual politics affect both the national identity of the nation of Uganda as well as the ecclesial identity of the Catholic (and Anglican, to an extent) Church in Uganda. I combined three important analytical

---

[14]Ibid., 1.

theories in this process: postcolonial, queer, and liberation theology.[15]

The foremost purpose of this work is to develop this research into a coherent approach toward ethics and AIDS that is in solidarity with those in the African and Afri-diasporic communities. That is to say, I research several sites where AIDS permeates and intersects with discourses of race, gender, and sexuality for and about African and African diasporic people. I will briefly discuss those issues in my final section regarding AIDSphobia. But this is a time of urgency. There is a "maafa"—a great catastrophe—out there! Many voices cry out in prayer and agony. And if we who theologize are not hearing these voices, are we not complicit to some degree in the pandemic, one fueled not only by an aggressive but non-conscious virus, but by the "virus" of ignorance, neocolonialism, homophobia, racism, and sexism orchestrated by a very conscious and ethically bankrupt Right(wing)?[16]

Exploring this situation, I also employ narrative criticism and deconstruction in a close reading of the 1886 Ugandan martyr-story. I want to explain how this story's "telling"—told and retold—manipulates the sexual politics and functions as

---

[15]I should say "post-Liberation Theology" because my critique includes both radical feminism and queer insights. Sex itself is the issue. Liberation Theology has been accused of being male dominated and silent about sex. Marcella Althaus-Reid, *Indecent Theology:Theological Perversions in Sex, Gender and Politics* (London: Routledge Press, 2000), 90.
[16]Maria Cimperman, *When God's People Have HIV/AIDS: An Approach to* Ethics (Maryknoll, N.Y.: Orbis Press), 11. "Virus" is a metaphor African ethicist Teresa Okure uses.

one of those crucial narratives of colonization and neocolonization.[17] I explore how "sodomitical discourse," in particular, was a necessary part of the West's domination over the "darkness" and "perdition" that the missionaries "discovered."[18] And I recognize, even today, that the European construction of sexuality has always coincided with the epoch of imperialism and that the two still inter-connect," as Mercer and Julien say above. That is, the age of imperialism has not ended, just changed.

For instance, the telling or theological framing of the Ugandan martyrdom and its antagonist, Mwanga II, continues to re-establish heteronormative dominating discourses. We will see how "sodomitical" discourse continues to function in present-day Ugandan state and church politics. In particular I draw on other African narratives and sources of homophobia as well as the Anglican Church's North vs. South struggle over homosexuality. Finally, we will look at how some traditional African sources can provide articulations for positive and inclusive approaches to AIDS in Africa.

---

[17]I, however, highly regard and honor Charles Lwanga and his Companions, as well as the profound faith and courage that they have engendered in Ugandan Catholics and Anglicans.

[18]By "sodomitical discourse," I refer to the demonization of male same-sex and gender variance that began in early redactions of the story of Sodom (and Gomorrah) in the Hebrew Scriptures (Genesis 19: 29-38), wherein rape of men is implied (Genesis 19: 4-5) and the city is thus destroyed by Yahweh for this and other sins.

I. The State of Homophobia and the Martyrs

Some estimates say that 95% of Ugandans oppose the legalization of homosexuality.[19] Open homosexual relationships are legally punishable by life imprisonment by law, but the law, until now, has not usually been applied. But agitation from a few vocal right wing segments, all usually connected with the churches, such as the Interfaith Rainbow Coalition against Homosexuality, keep alive the threats and force public officials to reaffirm their commitment to "crack down." Journalists risk their lives when they try to evenly report on the state of homosexual rights and AIDS prevention.[20]

The martyrs have been invoked today to attack gay, lesbian, bisexual, transgender, transsexual, intersexed, and questioning persons (glbttiq), represented in groups like Gays and Lesbians of Uganda (GALA), Musla-Uganda, and Sexual Minorities of Uganda (SMUG). This also includes attacks on the Anglican glbttiq group, Integrity Uganda" and its leader, retired Anglican bishop Christopher Senyonjo, as well as supportive scholars such as Sylvia Tamale and Ali Mazrui of Makerere University. "Safe houses" (or places of torture),

---

[19]Based on a Steadman Group poll reported at "Behind the Mask," http://www.mask.org.za/article.php?cat=uganda&id=1674 (Accessed July 9, 2009).

[20] These facts are recorded on the website "Behind the Mask." Regarding the threatened journalists, see in this same source the Stanford University student journalist who was "under fire in Uganda for covering gay issues." http://www.mask.org.za/article.php?cat=AfricaAbroad&id=1690. (Accessed October 9, 2008).

jailings, and rape of openly non-heterosexual people is still prevalent both in Uganda and the continent.[21] Homophobic hate speech from ecclesial and civic leaders, among others, is allowed to drown out any voice of moderation.

Homophobic rhetoric, rooted in sodomitical discourse from the past, has appropriated the telling of the martyrs' story, and has redrawn it into a wider discourse in post-colonial Africa. As such, the martyrs have been assumed into a venomous anti-homosexual national rhetoric [and policy] regarding what it means to be an authentic African. And that is frightening.

II. The Anglican Crisis

This bleak scenario is exacerbated by public statements of African Catholic bishops that maintain the traditional, strict teaching condemning condom use and includes scenes like that of (the late) Cardinal Outunga of Kenya burning condoms and safer sex materials.[22] Further, the Ugandan Anglican bishops, alienated by the easing of restrictions on homosexuality at the Lambeth Conference in 1998 and the ordination of openly-gay bishop Gene Robinson of New

---

[21]Regarding "safe houses" as places of torture, the source is a personal interview by the author with Christopher Kalema of Musla-Uganda, Makerere University, Uganda, October 30, 2004. Beatings, rapes, and arrests of gay, lesbian, and transgendered Africans are recorded on the website "Behind the Mask.org." http://www.mask.org.za/ (Accessed August 21, 2009).

[22]*New Vision (Kampala) September 29, 2003*. "Behind the Mask," October 7, 2004.

Hampshire, keep alive the threat of schism.[23] In March, 2005 Ugandan archbishop, Henry Luke Orombi, though he has said he is willing to "listen to views on the homosexuality debate in the Anglican Church," issued a joint communiqué with other Anglican prelates calling on the U.S. and Canadian churches to "voluntarily withdraw their members from the Anglican Consultative Council for the period leading up to the…Lambeth Conference," an international Anglican gathering held in 2008.[24] The request was intended to avoid confrontation over the issue of homosexuality and the possible result of schism. The Anglican Ugandan church is most outspoken on the issue of homosexuality.[25] The story of the Anglican bishop in one of Uganda's districts worst hit by AIDS—the Kasese district—is a striking example. According to the *Washington Post*, Jackson Nzerebende Tembo, Anglican bishop of the South Rwenzori Diocese, which serves the Kasese District, refused a large donation of money and the offer of physicians from the Episcopal Diocese of Central Pennsylvania, headquartered in Harrisburg, because it voted "yes" on the election of Bishop Robinson.[26]

---

[23]Kevin Ward, "Same-Sex Relations in Africa and the Debate on Homosexuality in East African Anglicanism." *Anglican Theological Review* vol. 34 no.1 (Winter 2002), 81.

[24]Jude Etyang and Jude Katende, "No Debate on Gays, says Orombi" New *Vision*, Kampala: Uganda (March 4, 2005). Henry Luke Orombi is the Anglican Archbishop of the Church of Uganda.

[25]See "Behind the Mask," http://www.mask.org.za/SECTIONS/AfricaPerCountry/ABC/uganda/uganda_84.htm. See also Etyang and Katende, *op cit*.

[26]From Colbert I. King, "A Tainted Easter Message," washingtonpost.com, 26 March 2005, A15.

Uganda, then, continues to be what Winston Churchill called it, the "pearl of Africa," not just in the imperialist, economic, and cultural sense Churchill meant but, indeed, as a discursive jewel. The martyr story continues to fuel many rightist agendas, be they strictly theo-ecclesial or geopolitical. In *Anglican Communion in Crisis: How Episcopal Dissidents and Their African Allies are Reshaping Anglicanism*, Anglican anthropologist Miranda Hassett argues that the larger scope of issues like homosexuality is the agenda(s) of the Western Right, which seeks, not without irony, to align itself with the African churches. This alliance is largely on the issue of homosexuality; the irony is that this same contingent helps to support neoliberal agendas that harm the global South. In Uganda there was always a "low church" or "evangelical" tradition in Anglicanism; orthodoxy was always measured by movements such as the Balokole or "saved ones."[27] These churches were, therefore, ripe for exploitation by the rightist global North; this is an example of Hassett's point, that the theological debate now takes place in a geopolitical locus.

> Conflicts over doctrine and morality within the Episcopal Church have been effectively globalized, so that they are now widely seen as of global, rather than domestic, scale and

[27]Miranda K. Hassett, *Anglican Communion in Crisis: How Episcopal Dissidents and Their African Allies are Reshaping Anglicanism* (Princeton: Princeton University Press, 2007), 27. This does not mean that this was all there was to the Church of Uganda. Pastorally speaking, for instance, the Church of Uganda, unlike its conservative Western counterparts, is responsible and deeply involved in the life of the whole person. Also, the Church of Uganda is more liberal regarding the role of women in leadership.

> significance. The North/South movement opposing Episcopal Church [USA] policies is both conservative and globalist....[28]

Not merely geopolitical, our own Ugandan martyr story is theo-political and, therefore, begs for a scholarly interdisciplinarity, a conversation, as it were, between martyrology, queer studies, Uganda political (colonial and postcolonial) history and progressive neocolonial studies.

III. Statement of the Problem: The "Telling" of the 1886 Bugandan Martyrdom.

Returning to our story, the narrative of the "passions" of the Uganda martyrs frames and overshadows the establishment of a regained manhood in both Ugandan Christianity and nationhood. It is not the sole establishment narrative at the cusp of colonial Ugandan history; moreover, it is not totally historical. It, however, sits as the most important story of colonial establishment and its very ahistorical "theological" character, as it were, allows it to cast a mythological or legendary shadow over Ugandan memory and identity that a strictly "historical" recounting could not. Its clothing in the language of martyrology is what makes it a theological metanarrative. It is this theological and ideological character that I am addressing when I stress the Ugandan martyrdom as a "telling" and a "retelling." I mean that through its narrative quality it establishes itself as the prime story of Christian spiritual ascendancy, and it does this over and over again, recasting itself in powerful and subtle ways. Indeed, in

---

[28]Ibid., 242.

each way it recasts itself it re-establishes that originating, engendering heteronormative text.

Importantly, this heteronormative telling and retelling of this story carries with it a canonized authority. The establishment of Christianity in Uganda—particularly Roman Catholic and Anglican Christianity—directly coincides with a narrative about transgressive same-sex desire. This makes for a provocative birth of Christianity in Eastern Africa: a "well-documented" account of so-called homosexual practice in Uganda that became "one of the defining events in the early history of Christianity in Uganda".[29] Furthermore, the subsequent 1964 canonization of the martyrs by Pope Paul VI further inscribes dark, dangerous desire into the skin of Christian Uganda. The canonization process is also a preached message; the narrative of the "martyrdom" becomes part of a canon of new narratives at the end of the nineteenth century: the ones about "sodomy," race, desire, and conquest. These are the "canons," as it were, of colonization.

IV. The Story Revisited, Reframed, Retold

This story remains powerful in Uganda—though, out of respect for the office of Kabaka, it remained hushed up until recently. But every time it is recast, it threateningly re-establishes that originating heteronormative Manichean plot of ultimate good vs. ultimate evil.

---

[29]Ward, 88.

a. Reframed as "Infamous Crime"

For example, the late Roman Catholic archbishop of New York, John Cardinal O'Connor, preaching on the subject of the Catholic priesthood in the modern day, referred to Pope Paul VI's 1964 homily of canonization of Charles Lwanga and his companions. The pope, he wrote, described the "homosexual advances" of Mwanga on the pages as a "crime si infâme"?[30] The pope's provocative, evocative words turn the memory of the event back towards this frame of "infamous crime," so that even theological notions like "they followed their faith" or "stood up for their faith" always means "denying the sexual trespass of an evil criminal."

Evil trespass is the point that O'Connor chose to keep alive in the minds of the priests he addressed. He continued in the tradition of many a Christian preacher who has attempted to scare out of the clergy any form of homosexuality, the inference being that there has been quite a bit of homosexuality to scare out of the clergy. Peter Damian, for example, was Prior of the community of hermits at Fonte Avellana in Italy from 1035-1043 and was responsible for coining the term *sodomia*. Damian was known to be a superb polemicist, who "from first to last… display[ed] a talent and a taste for attack," and regarded himself as a "writer of

---

[30]Cardinal John O'Connor, "Ministry for Priests in the Current Circumstances." (Vatican: The Holy See), http://www.vatican.va/roman_curia/congregations/cclergy/documents/rc_con_cclergy_doc (Accessed March 8, 2003).

persuasions rather than of histories."[31] He took the righteous role of one who was exposing an "abomination." Damian's disgusted tone and sophistry enlarged the importance of sodomy from that of a simple vice to a matter of faith and a doctrine of life and death.

b. Reframed as "Development"

Moreover, Paul VI uses the martyrdom to expand on the meaning of the famous notion of "development." This is done in the way the martyrs, in his description, become fighters and figures for "conscience" and "development." In his homily of canonization, Paul VI expands on the meaning of the "crime si infame" of Namugongo:

> It shows us by sufficiently manifest reasons that *new people* [emphasis added] need a moral foundation, to affirm new spiritual habits[,] to transmit [this moral foundation] to [their] posterity; this crime expresses almost symbolically and puts into action the *passage* [emphasis added] of a simple and rough way of life[—] where remarkable human values were not missing[,] but which [were] soiled and weakened, and enslaved to itself—towards a more civilized life in which prevail higher expressions of the human spirit [as well as] better social living conditions.[32]

---

[31]Mark D. Jordan, *The Invention of Sodomy in Christian Theology* (Chicago: The University of Chicago Press, 1997), 45-46.

[32]Pope Paul VI, *Apostolic Exhortation* (Vatican City, Italy, 1964), 56, 906. Brackets are mine.

Here Paul VI set Africa in an evangelizing speech that implied violence. In reducing the same-sex politics in the royal court to "crime" he evoked the balance of crime: punishment. This idea of crime shadows and complicates the canonization. That is to say, the shadow of "crime and punishment" muddies the aim of the canonization, which is to sublimate, spiritualize, sanitize, and silence this story of taboo sex.[33]

> The martyrdom…is fraught with drama…something which distresses us but…the injustice and violence…tend to fade from human memory, while before the eyes of succeeding generations there remains ever present the shining example of meekness which has transformed the laying down of life into a propitiatory sacrifice…a message continually handed on to the men of today and tomorrow.[34]

He, further, associated the blood of the martyrs with that which opens a "new epoch" in Africa. For Paul VI, the martyrdom fulfilled Africa's silent destiny, its "predisposition" to Christianity and its "[proper] vocation,"

---

[33]A logical, albeit non-theological, understanding would ask that if punishment is what the "criminal" deserves, why are the martyrs punished…since the storytellers and witnesses go out of their way to say that none of the canonized *ever* engaged in such sex?

[34]Pope Paul VI, in his 1964 canonization discourse, English translation issued by Fides Service. Quoted in Faupel (London: Geoffrey Chapman, 1965), 225.

making it part of the "mysterious design of God."[35] "The martyred are those who are the exceptions to the rule, who somehow rise above their own people's debasement. The new epoch that the Ugandan martyrdom inaugurated was a new national consciousness and religious identity. As icons of Christian identity, and paragons of sanctity, the martyrs represented a "new people" in need of a "moral foundation" that can lead the former Buganda away from its "soiled," "weakened," and "enslaved" past into a "more civilized life," that is to say, a "whiter,"[36] purer, "straighter" life.

Pope Paul VI, finally, referred to the martyrs as those "who sprang from the living trunk of African history to become the first fruits of Christian holiness in modern Africa."[37] The use of procreative (hetero) language supercedes the homosexually-charged events of 1886, transforming it, with a phrase, into a heterosexual spectacle. He referred to the blood of the martyrs as the "seed" planted in the fertile ground of Africa.[38]

---

[35]Faupel, *African Holocaust*, 225.

[36]Thus, the martyrs-become-(almost) white themselves.

[37]I first saw this fragment of Paul VI's 1964 homily published in a 2001 diocesan newsletter for the Black Catholics of Oakland sent by Dr. Toinette Eugene in preparation for the upcoming June 3 celebration of Martyrs Day. This phrase, therefore, shapes how American Black Catholics heard the story.

[38]This quote contains a language of development springing forth from the sexual language of fertility…a hetero or natural fertility borne despite the non-fertile ground of male-male sodomy. This is not to take the pope's words literally. Rather, it is to see how words and language in general, work in their own way to frame, in this case, Africa and the martyrdom.

Such "word plays" might seem far-fetched, but the case of the Ugandan martyrs exists, as a metanarrative, in a liminal zone between language and representation. In these above examples, for instance, the martyrdom becomes a cautionary tale for contemporary priests, a case for development, and a "seminal" source for theological development.

V. Who was/is this Mwanga?

Kabaka Mwanga has been called "Africa's most famous homosexual."[39] The fact that he, like all royals, had wives and children is ignored. Moreover, although he—and this is important—was the same age as many of the pages, he is cast as a "pedophile" in the modern fiction of a "dirty old man," a predator. And although we know that same-sex activity was present in the court, it was Mwanga's (as king) "shameful passions" that were zeroed in upon, leaving the rest of the royal court in rumor. Did he get "it" from the Muslims in the court? How did he abuse the other pages? What was he like? Was he effeminate? The texts tag him in various negative ways:

> A man with a weak-looking mouth, and a rather silly sort of laugh and smile; he raises his eyebrows very high, and twitches them in surprise, or in giving assent to a statement. He looked a young and frivolous sort of man, very weak and easily led; passionate and, if provoked, petulant.

---

[39]Ward, 88.

> He looked as if he would be easily frightened, and possessed of very little courage or self-control.[40]

But what of the other admittedly prurient questions? How prevalent was same-sex practice in the court? What place does it play in the overall sexual politics of the court? Can one "get" desire, "catch" desire from someone else (e.g., Arab traders)? If that's not possible, is it not then within the realm of possibility that same-sex desire (along with other sexual desires and practices) is pre-Arab, pre-European?[41] Is it possible that there were other "gender variant," effeminate men or masculine women in the country before the missionaries exposed them? These are the honest questions about sexuality that metanarratives like this one obscure. What were the love relationships of the other men? What about the romance and the triangles between men, between women and men, and between women? What did the missionaries know of this practice from Europe? (e.g.: Could we infer that the missionaries also "knew" about the Orientalist contention of Arab sodomy?) And, what of the non-sexual intrigue and real threats of European colonization that stirred up all this tension?

---

[40]Faupel, *African Holocaust*, 67.

[41]There, actually, is a growing body of scholarship that points to the existence of same-sex, gender variant practice and roles in pre-colonial Africa. See, for instance, Murray, Stephen O. and Will Roscoe. *Boy-wives and Female Husbands: Studies in African Homosexualities.* (New York: St. Martin's Press, 2001). The problem, again, is not so much that such practices existed/s, but how to understand the meaning they held and hold in various African cultures. And, of course, racism and colonialism have served to muddy the scene, making it difficult to even speak on the subject.

But since Mwanga's so-called homosexuality is most useful to the European missionaries, explorers, and entrepreneurs--and since he obliged them by carrying out the bloody executions--Mwanga is, indeed, Africa's most famous homosexual. Indeed, Mwanga, years after losing the kingdom of Buganda to British colonial forces, is still a stereotype, his name a noun and adjective for a predatory sodomite.[42] An article in the *New Vision*, one of Uganda's leading daily newspapers, by a Ugandan Christian pastor named Martin Ssempa is revealing.[43] For him, Mwanga is the personification of any non-African, anti-God "agenda." He speaks of this agenda as a "gradual global Mwanga" that is spreading across the world and destroying Christian societies and families, particularly in Africa. He had his own "personal Mwanga experience with a famous Ugandan" (whom he describes but does not name) who offered him a job only if he would have sex with him. A "personal Mwanga" from his point of view is, evidently, a predatory male, or any man who makes a pass at him.

VI. Wheyting Be Dat? The Homosexual in Non-theological African Narrative.

African scholar Chris Dunton's groundbreaking essay, "Wheyting be Dat? The Treatment of Homosexuality in

---

[42]Though, of course, this is not from all sources, such as those who do not wish to throw aspersions on the Kabakas.

[43]Martin Ssempa, "When Faith, State, and State-inspired Homosexuality Clash." *New Vision, June 3, 2005.* http://www.newvision.co.ug/D/8/459/437768.

African Literature”[44], questions the assumptions and the “unsaying” (or denials) of African homosexuality by “post-colonial” (i.e, after colonial times) African writers.[45] These unsayings—seen in public pronouncements of African politicians and clergy—construct Africa as patriarchal and heteronormative and assume that homosexuality and effeminacy are part of the racism and colonial oppression internalized by, in Frantz Fanon’s term, the “Negrophobic man.”[46]

In general, “homosexuality” is presented in post-colonial speech as a rupture in traditional African mores. It is supposedly exposed as a colonialist plot, and the homosexual’s personal identity is brought forward in this plot.[47] The title “Wheyting be dat?” refers to a line asked by a puzzled grandmotherly character in the African play, *Big Berrin*, by Yulissa A Maddy. The grandmother asks,

---

[44]Chris Dunton, “'Wheyting be Dat?': The Treatment of Homosexuality in African Literature,” *Research in African Literature* vol. 20 no. 3 (Fall 1989): 422-448.

[45]Marc Epprecht, “The 'Unsaying' of Indigenous Homosexualities in Zimbabwe: Mapping a Blindspot in an African Masculinity,” *Journal of Southern African Studies* 24/4 (Dec. 1998) 631-51.

[46]This is psychiatrist and postcolonial theorist Frantz Fanon’s expression connecting the self-hatred of African men with repressed homosexual tendencies. Frantz Fanon, *Black Skin, White Masks* (New York: Grove Press, 1967), 156.

[47]Guarav Desai, “Out in Africa,” in *Postcolonial, Queer: Theoretical Intersections,* ed. John Hawley (Albany: State University of New York Press, 2001), 140-41.

"Homosexuality? Wheyting [what] be dat?"[48] Dunton's point is that homosexuality is still depicted in the great majority of texts as either unknown or as a stigmatized "'un-African' activity." These texts most often depict African homosexuality in negative ways: as confused and deeply colonized men and women, as traitors to African identity, as "spectacularly effeminate," as pimp-cum-menservants, as lesbians providing "exotic relief," and, as in our case from Buganda, as "predators" and "pedophiles." Moreover, some modern African literature continues the plots that "[enact]...elaborate symbolic executions...."[49]

Many of these writers, however, at least understand the complexity of issues around sexuality and gender in Africa.[50] Theologians can learn from literature to step back and look at our own narrative strategies and then transpose our idealism into plots. Narrative theology, in fact, is the better way to approach sexual complexities. As the late Mujerista thea/ologian, Marcella Althaus-Reid, taught, developing a theology of "sex stories" expands the interpretation and understanding of the complex subjects of theology.[51] Such a

---

[48]Chris Dunton, "'Wheyting?" 423.

[49]Ibid., 424.

[50]Of Ama Ata Aidoo's novel, *Our Sister Killjoy*, for instance, Dunton wrote that when in African literature homosexuality "becomes liberated [it] is granted a greater capacity to disturb" (Dunton, 423).

[51]Marcella Althaus-Reid, *Indecent Theology: Theological Perversions in Sex, Gender and Politics* (London: Routledge Press, 2000). Althaus-Reid, who died in February of 2009, might also be called a pioneer of sexual

hermeneutic allows us to discover that there are more stories than categories, expanding Christian theology and ethics, which are both, she feels, presently lacking in imagination and power.[52] For Althaus-Reid, all theology contains the elements of some sexual narrative, be it the procreativity or creativity of high systematics or the inside stories of the secret spiritual lives of Christian ancestors, clerics, religious, or of theologians themselves.[53] Knowing that these sexual stories are different, complex, and often very difficult helps the theologian and ethicist complete necessary hermeneutical circles.

VII. Facing AIDSphobia and Human Rights

AIDS is, in the words of cultural worker Jan Zita Grover, a "360-degree sense-surround," and "there is no door out of it leading back."[54] Both theoretically and theologically speaking, that hoped-for "door leading back" refers to the old comfortable positions of "normalcy," of stable straight family identities, of old political coalitions and nationalisms, and of

---

theology, especially "queer theology." Liberation Theology, she held, must be transformed by both feminist and queer theologies.

[52]Ibid., 132.

[53]See, for instance, Virginia Burrus' discussion of the "erotics of ancient hagiography" in *The Sex Lives of Saints: The Erotics of Ancient Hagiography* (Philadelphia: University of Pennsylvania Press, 2004).

[54]David Woodhead, "HIV, Space, and the Constitution of Identities" in *Mapping Desire: Geographies of Sexualities*, ed. David Bell and Gill Valentine (London: Routledge Press, 1995), 231-44.

the abomination rhetoric and tired patriarchal condemnations of "indecency." But that way is closed. That is the way of AIDSphobia.

Queer theorist and black speculative fiction writer Samuel R. Delany believes that HIV/AIDS is that phenomenon through which, into which, so many other discourses now pass. It is a matrix. In his essay "The Rhetoric of Sex/The Discourse of Desire" he writes:

> [HIV/AIDS]...is certainly the largest material factor in the transformation of the discourse of desire and that transformation's manifestation is the rhetoric of sex...for AIDS has come as close to unifying certain strands of sexual discourse as it has come to fraying certain others.[55]

Delany's observation is what grounds AIDS theory, a theory that demands the most radical and honest of critiques. By "radical" I refer to a materialist interruption to the erotophobic, somatophobic, and idealist strains found in much of Roman Catholic sexual ethics.[56] That is, I am looking at the

---

[55]Samuel R. Delany, "Out in Africa," in his collection, *Shorter Views: Queer Thoughts & the Politics of the Paraliturgy* (Hanover, N.H.: Weslayan University Press, 1999), 34.

[56]Somatophobia is defined as fear of pleasure and fear of the body, the latter being essentially associated, according to much of radical sex feminist theology and exegesis, with the woman. See Aline Rousselle, *Porneia* (Oxford: Blackwell, 1988); Bernadette J. Brooten, *Love Between Women* (Chicago: University of Chicago Press, 1996); Ross Shepard Kraemer, *Her Share of the Blessings: Women's Religions Among Pagans, Jews and Christians in the Greco-Roman World* (Oxford: Oxford University, 1992); Virginia Burrus, "Word in Flesh: The Bodies and

effect of the dominant Christian theological narrative on the bodies and spirits of Africans. This task is daunting; but the discursive, symbolic opportunities are great.

Presently, the condemnation of homosexuality, condoms, and the privileging of marital sex and chastity (abstinence only) places the burden of the spread of AIDS on hidden sexual practices—often men having sex with men; and most often women carrying the burden of the disease in their bodies often due to the hidden (often same-sex) behavior of their husbands.[57] AIDS activists in Africa claim that the denial of the reality of men-having-sex-with-men has skewed even HIV information campaigns. Indeed, one source even claims that "heterosexist approaches to HIV prevention campaigns have actually led some people to believe that anal sex is safe and that gay sex does not require protection."[58] There are still complaints of a horrible lack of attention on the part of the government to treating the disease in the LGBT community in Uganda.

Sexualities of Ascetic Women in Christian Antiquity" in *Diacritics* 28.2 (1998): 52.

[57]Neil McKenna, *The Silent Epidemic: HIV/AIDS and Men Who Have Sex with Men in the Developing World (London: Panos, 1999),* *http://ww.panos.org.uk/images/books/* This is seen in the truck driver culture in Zimbabwe and elsewhere, where men bring HIV/AIDS back home. I personally conducted an interview in 2003 with HIV+ Patricia Vito, whose husband had given her AIDS, and (later on) a number of activists in Gays and Lesbians of Zimbabwe (GALZ) who witnessed this sad phenomenon.

[58]Author interview with "Daniel," Info@mask.org.za, (March 7, 2005).

These attitudes regarding the un-African-ness of homosexuality and the insistence on a pure heterosexual identity for Africa affects the way AIDS is seen and not seen, the way it is transmitted and treated. AIDS theory in Africa is receiving increasingly significant notice and treatment by African scholars. AIDS becomes central to African queer scholarship specifically because the continent, perhaps more than anywhere else, has to pass through a sieve of demonization or denial of same-sex practice, legalized homophobia, secrecy, and, now, neo-colonialism. Moreover, the basic constructions that frame the discussions about "homosexuality" or "AIDS in Africa" are filled with racist fictions rigged by the West.[59] And so homophobia and heterosexism hold much responsibility for AIDS deaths in Africa.

African scholars like Chris Dunton and Mai Palmberg warned about the danger in identifying the "curse" of HIV/AIDS with homosexuality, because such identification is "not only ill-informed, it is dangerous, as it obscures real knowledge about the disease and muddles any practical awareness as to how to deal with it."[60] Their argument against homophobia, then, is both humanitarian and pragmatic; that is, it understands the ethical and the actual material byproducts of homophobic discourse for effected or affected Africans.

---

[59]See, for instance, Cindy Patton's "Inventing African AIDS," *Inventing AIDS*. New York: Routledge, 1990.

[60]Chris Dunton and Mai Palmberg, "Human Rights and Homosexuality in Southern Africa." *Current African Issues* 19 (Uppsala, Sweden: The Nordic Africa Institute, 1996), 28.

The questions remain: Can Africans create resistance to heteronormativity? “Are gay rights a part of human rights?”[61] How can we find solidarity with Africa in this ongoing crisis? The solutions are complex, but perhaps one answer to these questions can be found in a surprising source: traditional African spirituality and religion.

Conclusion: The Return of Nende

An article reprinted on the website “Dispatches from the Vanishing World,” entitled “The Gods Break Through in Uganda: The Nende Files”, reports the 1997 visit of the progressive late Ugandan Catholic theologian Fr. John Mary Waliggo to Nsambya Hospital, Kampala.[62] He interviewed Sister Nelizinho Carhalho, a heroic nun who started the first blood-screening program in AIDS-ravaged Kampala. While there, the characteristics of the god Nende were recalled: a god of “plague attacks…sleeping sickness….”[63] One of the priests at the hospital then said, “We would like a god of AIDS.” His words are an invocation and an implied invitation to Nende, or to Kawimpule, the god of bubonic plague, or to the goddess

---

[61]Ibid., 8.

[62]*Lapis* Magazine, “The Gods Break Through in Uganda: The Nende Files,” *Dispatches from the Vanishing World. The Reader's Website Dedicated to Preserving Species and Culture* Issue 4 (Spring 1997), http://www.dispatchesfromthevanishingworld.com/pastdispatches/uganda/uganda1.html (Accessed August 19, 2009).

[63]Brother Tarcis A Nsobya, *The African Heroes* (Kibusi: Mirianum Press, 1999), 10.

Mukasa, protectress of the procreated, to return and serve the African people in this time of AIDS. The interesting thing is that the Ugandan martyrs were burned facing Nende, the god they supposedly insulted.[64] Charles Lwanga had been dedicated to the goddess of Lake Victoria and procreation, Mukasa. It is said that, before his conversion to Christianity, Charles Lwanga was "determined to be a priest to the god Mukasa."[65] Interrupting the heteronormative telling of the martyrs' story can be not only a contemporary contribution to understanding how this story writes itself upon the bodies of Africans today, it also can serve to present a new template, a new close reading and interpretation of the story. The martyrs become the patrons of a new understanding of sex, sexual ethics, and those populations and persons affected by AIDS.

What is important about Nende and so many African and Afri-diasporic deities, or orishas, is the non-condemnatory nature, indeed the sex-positive positions, of so many of them. For glbttiq persons in Africa, there is indeed great potential and power in the return of gay-friendly ancestors and of various gender-variant orishas. Most important is that these are African divinities. Africa is their home—wherever "Africa" travels, across whatever oceans or plains or eras, they go too.

Later that afternoon, after visiting with the sick of the Kampala hospital, Fr. Waliggo invited the reporter of the story

---

[64]Loiuse Pirouet, *Strong in the Faith: The Witness of the Uganda Martyrs* (Mukono, Uganda: Church of Uganda Literature Centre, 1969), 41.

[65]Nsobya, 10.

in "Dispatches from the Vanishing World" to tea. Reportedly, Waliggo was asked "Are the old gods alive for the Baganda, now that most are devout Christians?" Waliggo responded: "How can they go? Where can they go? They are part and parcel of us."

WORKS CITED

Althaus-Reid, Marcella. *Indecent Theology: Theological Perversions in Sex, Gender and Politics*. London: Routledge Press, 2000.

Behind the Mask. http://www.mask.org.za/.

Bleys, Rudi C. *The Geography of Perversion: Male-to-Male Sexual Behavior Outside the West and the Ethnographic Imagination, 1750-1918*. New York: New York University Press, 1995.

Boisvert, Donald. L. *Sanctity and Male Desire: A Gay Reading of Saints*. Cleveland: Pilgrim Press, 2004.

Cimperman, Maria. *When God's People Have HIV/AIDS: An Approach to Ethics*. Maryknoll, N.Y.: Orbis Press, 2005.

Conner, Randy. *Blossom of Bone: Reclaiming the Connections Between Homoeroticism and the Sacred.* San Francisco: Harper Press, 1993.

Delany, Samuel R. "The Rhetoric of Sex/The Discourse of Desire." In *Shorter Views: Queer Thoughts & the Politics of the Paraliturgy*. Hanover, N.H.: Wesleyan University Press, 1999.

Desai, Guarav. "Out in Africa." In *Postcolonial, Queer: Theoretical Intersections*, edited by John Hawley, 139-64. Albany: State University of New York Press, 2001.

Dunton, Chris. "Wheyting be Dat?" The Treatment of Homosexuality in African Literature." *Research in African Literature.* vol.. 20, No.3, Fall 1989.

Dunton, Chris, and Mai Palmberg. "Human Rights and Homosexuality in Southern Africa." *Current African Issues* 19. Uppsala, Sweden: The Nordic Africa Institute, 1996.

Ellison, Marvin and Judith Plaskow, eds. *Heterosexism in Contemporary World Religion: Problem and Prospect.* Cleveland: Pilgrim Press, 2007.

Epprecht, Marc. "The 'Unsaying' of Indigenous Homosexualities in Zimbabwe: Mapping a Blindspot in an African Masculinity." *Journal of Southern African Studies.* 24/4 (Dec. 1998): 631-51.

Fanon, Frantz. *Black Skin, White Masks*. New York: Grove Press, 1967.

Faupel, J. F. *African Holocaust: The Story of the Ugandan Martyrs*. New York: P. J. Kenedy and Sons, 1962.

Faupel, J. F. *African Holocaust: The Story of the Ugandan Martyrs*. London: Geoffrey Chapman, 1965.

Greer, Allan. "Iroquois Virgin: The Story of Catherine Tekawitha in New France and New Spain." In *Colonial Saints: Discovering the Holy in the Americas, 1500-1800*, edited by Allan Greer and Jodi Bilinkoff, 235-50. New York: Routledge Press, 2003.

Hassett, Miranda K. *Anglican Communion in Crisis: How Episcopal Dissidents and Their African Allies are Reshaping Anglicanism*. Princeton: Princeton University Press, 2007.

Hawley, John, ed. *Postcolonial, Queer: Theoretical Intersections.* Albany: State University of New York Press, 2001.

Hoad, Neville. *African Intimacies: Race, Homosexuality, and Globalization*. Minneapolis: University of Minnesota Press, 2007.

Jordan, Mark D. *The Invention of Sodomy in Christian Theology*. Chicago: The University of Chicago Press, 1997.

Lapis Magazine. "The Gods Break Through in Uganda: The Nende Files." *Dispatches from the Vanishing World. The Reader's Website Dedicated to Preserving Species and Culture*. Issue 4, Spring 1997. http://www.dispatchesfromthevanishingworld.com/pastdispatches/uganda/uganda1.html (Accessed August 20, 2009).

Lowe, D. A. *Buganda in Modern History.* Berkeley: University of California Press, 1971.

Massad, Joseph A. *Desiring Arabs*. Chicago: University of Chicago Press, 2008.

McKenna, Neil. *The Silent Epidemic: HIV/AIDS and Men Who Have Sex with Men in the Developing World.* London: Panos, 1999. http://www.panos.org.uk/images/books/THE%20SILENT%20EPIDEMIC.pdf (Accessed October 15, 2006).

Murray, Stephen O. and Will Roscoe. *Boy-wives and Female Husbands: Studies in African Homosexualities.* New York: St. Martin's Press, 2001.

Nsobya, Brother Tarcis A (Munnakaroli). *The African Heroes*. Kibusi: Marianum Press, 1999.

O'Connor, John, Cardinal. "Ministry for Priests in the Current Circumstances." http://www.vatican.va/roman_curia/congregations/cclergy/documents/rc_con_cclergy_doc. (Accessed March 8, 2003).

Paul VI, Pope. *Apostolic Exhortation* 56, 906. Vatican City, Italy. 1964.

---. "Eucharistic Celebration at the Conclusion of the Symposium Organized by the Bishops of Africa." Kampala, Uganda. July 13, 1969.

---. "Homily in Honor of the Martyrs of Uganda." Sunday October 18, 1964.

---. "Let There Be Peace in Africa." *Leadership: Souvenir Issue*. September-October 1969. No. 129: 19-25. Kampala, Uganda.

---. "*Populorum Progressio*: Encyclical of Pope Paul VI on the Development of Peoples." March 26, 1967. Available at http://www.vatican.va/holy_father/paul_vi/encyclicals/documents/hf_p-vi_enc_26031967_populorum_en.html. (Accessed February 7, 2007).

---. "To the Heart of Africa." *The Pope Speaks*. Vol. 14. 1969.

Pirouet, Louise. *Strong in the Faith: The Witness of the Uganda Martyrs*. Mukono, Uganda: Church of Uganda Literature Centre, 1969.

Ssempa, Martin. "When Faith, State, and State-inspired Homosexuality Clash." *New Vision*. http://www.newvision.co.ug/D/8/459/437768/martin%20ssempa June 3, 2005.

Thoonen, J.P. *Black Martyrs*. New York: Sheed and Ward, 1941.

Ward, Kevin. "Same-Sex Relations in Africa and the Debate on Homosexuality in East African Anglicanism." *Anglican Theological Review*. 34.1 (Winter 2002): 81-111.

Woodhead, David. "HIV, Space, and the Constitution of Identities." In *Mapping Desire: Geographies of Sexualities*, edited by David Bell, and Gill Valentine, 231-44. London: Routledge Press, 1995.

BOOK REVIEWS

BETWEEN BARACK AND A HARD PLACE: RACISM AND WHITE DENIAL IN THE AGE OF OBAMA by *Tim Wise*. Pp. 160. City Lights Publishers, San Francisco, California, 2009. $13.95. ISBN: 978-0872865006 (paper).

Tim Wise, writer, lecturer, economist, political analyst, and anti-racist popular speaker has written three major books on race in America or to put it more succinctly how white Americans consider themselves superior to people who are blacks, native Americans, Latinos, Asians, and non-whites of European descent. As whites they take for granted that they will win and that they will succeed. Wise concurs that the election of Obama is of the greatest importance, but this does not mean that racism is now over. He has put it this way: "Is white America really ready for a black president?" Tim Wise answers in his book that it is not.

For Wise there are two forms of racism which have resulted from this election. First, according to Wise, there is the old-fashioned bigotry or simple racism. Wise calls it Racism 1.0. Blacks and browns (to use his terms), are well acquainted in our society. Call it systemic racial discrimination, traditional forms of segregation, vivid memoriea of lynching, race rioting, and maintenance of well-known areas, privately developed, and closed to blacks. This type of racism rejected Obama from the very beginning and still lurks in the hearts and minds of many whites.

On the other hand, Obama won because there were enough whites from whom there had emerged a certain "enlightened exceptionalism," which he calls Racism 2.0. These considered Obama as "having 'transcended' [his] blackness in some way." It is this form of racism that is now alive and well in the United States. Wise lists the many social institutions that have broken down among blacks and people of color: education, housing, the criminal justice system. Once again, this is the broken down areas in Racism 1.0. An example was the situation of blacks and non-whites during the flooding in New Orleans during *Katrina.* Consider not only looting and the plight of the aged and the frail, neglected and abandoned, but also the groups of blacks who were barred by white inhabitants from crossing a bridge into an adjacent section of the city. They were armed with weapons. "At least eleven men, all black, were shot by whites in the days following the flooding…" (p. 70)

Wise's conclusion is that Obama was able to win the approval of many educated whites who were able to "transcend" incidents in racism, because Obama seemed to go beyond "black issues." And many whites were able to support him. A recent incident of "profiling" of Henry Gates in Cambridge by a policeman did momentarily raise the president's ire.

Tim Wise comes to the conclusion that whites must take responsibility for the transformation of racism and privilege to justice and equality. Perhaps one may add that, despite everything, we who are blacks have the responsibility for sharing with Obama a new and different vision. As he said in his inauguration address: "…we cannot help but believe that the old hatreds shall someday pass; that the lines of tribe shall soon dissolve…"

CYPRIAN DAVIS, O.S.B.
SAINT MEINRAD ARCHABBEY
SAINT MEINRAD, INDIANA 47577

MY GRANDFATHER'S SON: A MEMOIR by Clarence Thomas. Pp. xiii + 292. HarperCollins, New York, 2007. $26.95 (cloth), $15.95 (paper). ISBN: 0060565551 (cloth), 978-0-06-056556-5 (paper).

The concept of one's identity, particularly one's racial identity, is complex and mediated by many factors. Our identity is not merely determined by family dynamics; where one is from; our time in history; how we think others see us and how we would like to be seen. Clarence Thomas's story is one filled with issues of identity, pain and struggle. His is a story of individual identity versus group identity; of race, inheritance, internal struggles with self doubt, change and transformation, and a loss of faith. His is the story of a black man's rise to high profile leadership positions, the power of association, and the experience of racial and religious heterodoxy. These and other related struggles and tensions make *My Grandfather's Son: A Memoir,* both an insightful and worthwhile read into the complexities of black identity.

For most readers this will be a venture from the known to the unknown world of Clarence Thomas, a one-time educated and professed Catholic who became Supreme Court Justice. While carrying a glossy hard cover copy of the book around in plain view, I thought of the review I should write based on lessons I learned from casual on-lookers and their unsolicited comments about the author. Initially any black Catholic reading Thomas might learn that it is risky to be seen in his company, even if only in print.

At times I found myself quickly explaining to others why I was reading *My Grandfather's Son*—explaining that I was indeed a faculty member at a nearby university and that I was thinking about using it for a class. Surely I was first and foremost an individual who should be able to read whatever and whomever I liked, without judgment. Not the case. I was a black man reading the story of a high profile ultra-conservative black man who represents to some what is inherently wrong with black folks who rise to the top. They are seen as elitists, haters of other black folks who cannot seem to get their act together, Uncle Toms, whitish blacks and sell-outs. In that regard, Thomas's story is not unique.

Thomas, a one-time professed Catholic, is sharing his story in his own words; for example, stories of individuals and events in his life that strongly influenced his transformation from a left-wing political liberal to a right-wing political conservative. He shares stories of disappointment that drove him from the larger Church. The stories of Thomas, who once believed that "the whole of the American culture was irretrievably tainted by racism" (p. 50), to the Thomas who later became one who rejected supportive programs that specifically targeted African Americans. These points of departure and their justification make his story a compelling read.

Thomas's accounts of his transformational years at Holy Cross and Yale Law School and his growing association and relationships with black conservatives like economists Thomas Sowell, Journalists, Juan Williams and Walter Williams, and Jay Parker (founder of the Lincoln Review), along with past presidents Ronald Reagan, George W. Bush and George H. W. Bush are thought-provoking. Although some of us might disagree with their right-wing political positions, and especially their positions on the significance of race, when we read about them we never fail to learn something deeply important about ourselves, even if only to affirm our own opposing positions to theirs. Like us, Thomas is greatly influenced by our setting and our associations.

Memoirs and autobiographies should be a particular draw and make a particular contribution to our understanding of the black experience in America and to our understanding of why some of us leave the Church for good. Nearly a century ago, black sociologist W.E.B. DuBois claimed that there is not enough known of the Negro experience in America. Memoirs offer a unique glimpse into the minds and hearts of those who write them. Theirs are sacred stories which offer insights into the author's search for truth and they reveal important life-changing experiences and events shared in their own words.

Dorothy Day wrote in her own 1952 memoir, *The Long Loneliness: The Autobiography of the Legendary Catholic Social Activist (HarperOne 1996)*, that, "When one writes the story of his life and the work he has been engaged in, it is a confession too, in a way" (p. 10). Thomas' establishes a confessional tone early when he writes,

> "It [his story] is the story of an ordinary man to whom extraordinary things happened. Putting it down on paper forced me to suffer old hurts, endure old pains, and revisit old doubts . . . Part of

> the reason for wanting to tell my story was to bear witness to what these people [my grandparents] did for me, though I also wanted to leave behind an accurate record of my own life as I remember it" (pp. ix-xii).

Thomas's story lies somewhere between Henry Louis Gate Jr.'s *Colored People: A Memoir (Vintage Press, 1995)* and Barack Obama's *Dreams from My Father: A Story of Race and Inheritance (Three Rivers Press, 2007)*, yet not in the same league as either. Like Gates, Thomas appears direct in sharing intimate family stories and painful encounters with his grandfather whom he called Daddy. Like Obama, Thomas barely knew his biological father and a grandparent played a major role in his formation in the Deep South. Although race and inheritance are not in the title of Thomas's book, they should be. His story, like Obama's, has everything to do with race, inheritance, identity, and a search for truth. Knowing that Thomas was a Catholic who was educated in Catholic schools through college was what initially drew me to his story.

The book could be divided into three parts. The first is a story of young Thomas and his early upbringing as a Catholic, first educated by Missionary Franciscan Sisters and later at Conception, a minor Seminary in Missouri where he flirted with the idea of becoming a priest. The second part begins with his experiences at Holy Cross College in Worcester, MA and the events that lead up to him walking out on mass halfway through and for the last time. It was at Holy Cross where he claims he had his first brush with "racial heterodoxy."

One would assume that Thomas' story would include more on his experience of being a black Catholic and how the Church informed his outlook on life. Unfortunately, Thomas spends much more time on why he left the Church rather than on what he believed as a Catholic. Thomas then shares with the reader the beginning events and people who influenced his conversion to a hard-line Republican.

The third and final part of the book focuses on Thomas' political career; his politically conservative associations and relationships; and last but not least his high profile confirmation hearing. Here he names his harshest political critics and frustrations that ultimately led him to accuse members of the Committee of a "high tech lynching . . . caricatured by a committee of the U.S. Senate rather than hung from a tree" (p. 271).

It is not to say that we should read every book written about or by a black person, however, we should take special note of those who have or are leaving a mark on history. Good, bad, or indifferent, we are them and they are us. *My Grandfather's Son: A Memoir* is indeed a worthwhile read if one is willing to take the risk of being seen with Clarence Thomas, even if only in print. Indeed, in the spirit of DuBois, we can never know enough of the black experience in America. Many of us can relate to this unlikely storyteller made famous by his controversial appointment to the highest court in the land and his memoir told only as he remembered it. His is a story of race, inheritance, identity, internal struggle with self doubt; pain; change; leadership; and a loss of faith in the broadest sense. His is a story of black identity in America.

ROBERT L. BARTLETT
AFRICANA EDUCATIONAL PROGRAM
EASTERN WASHINGTON UNIVERSITY
CHENEY, WA 99004-2428

UNCOMMON FAITHFULNESS: THE BLACK CATHOLIC EXPERIENCE, edited by *M. Shawn Copeland, with LaReine-Marie Mosely SND,* and *Albert Raboteau (with contributions by Diane Batts Morrow, Cyprian Davis OSB, Cecilia Moore, Katrina M. Samuels, Jamie T. Phelps OP, Diana L. Hayes, Bryan N. Massingale, Archbishop Wilton D. Gregory, Kevin P. Johnson, Paulinus I. Odozor CSSp, and Clarence Williams CPPS).* Pp. xii + 221. Orbis Books, Maryknoll, New York, 2009. $26.00. ISBN: 978-1570758195 (paper).

From the time Christianity emerged nearly two millennia ago there have been peoples who, in the midst of oppression and injustice, have looked beyond their present realities toward the light of Christ and the message of the New Testament. *Uncommon Faithfulness* highlights the vision and accomplishments of African Americans who have done this very thing in the face of subjugation, racism, and other forms of oppression and neglect by exploring the ways in which their experiences have shaped and strengthened their faith.

Uncommon Faithfulness is an edited collection of papers delivered during the March 2004 conference of the same title hosted by The Cushwa Center for the Study of American Catholicism of the University of Notre Dame. Divided into three major sections – History, Theological and Ethical Reflection, and Pastoral Concerns – this collection explores the faith of those whom society, and even the Church, had abandoned, or, at best, relegated to the position of second-class citizens. An important contribution to the scholarship of blacks in the Church, *Uncommon Faithfulness* features the work of some of the most prominent theologians, historians, and pastoral ministers of our era, as well as a few relative newcomers to the academy. For those who desire a spotlight on modern black Catholic scholarship, *Uncommon Faithfulness* provides excellent insight into some of the most pressing issues facing African American Catholics today.

The *History* section explores the shaping forces of race and religion on the lives of African Americans. The work of Albert Raboteau opens this section with an analysis of African American religion based on religious narratives. From the slave narratives, to the Congresses lead by Daniel Rudd, to the work of Howard Thurman and James Baldwin, Raboteau presents four models reflecting the major ways in which African Americans have – and continue to – view religion through the lens of race. Raboteau's article is followed by two historical essays on the origins of two African American religious communities, the Oblate Sisters of Providence (Diane Batts Morrow) and the Sisters of the Holy Family (Cyprian Davis OSB). Batts Morrow describes the challenges faced by the Oblate Sisters of Providence as they struggled to form a religious community of black women despite "clerical disapproval of the concept of a black sisterhood" (p. 29). Suffering for nearly four years from the neglect of diocesan authorities after the death of their spiritual director, they survived as a community through devotion to God and to community life, and the hope that goodness would prevail over racism, indifference, and disdain. Next Davis presents a similar story of success against the odds, viewed through a look at the life of Henriette DeLille, founder of the Sisters of the Holy Family. This small group of black women dedicated themselves to God and served the community by teaching young black girls and ministering to the sick and dying. Cecilia Moore's article on the desegregation of the Diocese of Raleigh, North Carolina, follows. Moore recounts the efforts of Bishop Vincent Waters to desegregate the churches and high schools of North Carolina while facing threats that many whites would withdraw financial support, leave their parishes or even the Catholic Church in general, and worst of all, provoke violence. For Waters, "Faith was the cure for racism" (p. 72), particularly faith expressed in the form of love for one's neighbor. Finally, the article of Katrina Sanders wraps up the *History* section with an analysis of the subtle ways in which black Catholic clergy supported the Civil Rights movement.

The next section, *Theological and Ethical Reflection*, features the work of M. Shawn Copeland, LaReine-Marie Mosely SND, Jamie T. Phelps OP, Diana Hayes, and Bryan Massingale. All five papers seek to answer these questions: How is the message of the Church articulated in the lived experiences of African Americans? How can the research and scholarship of the Church help guide Catholics toward the message of the New Testament? Copeland explores the message of Blues music and the way it captures the pain, sorrow, hope and faith of African Americans. She analyzes the imagery of the crossroads in Blues tradition and the ways it symbolizes the cross of Jesus. Mosely presents the ways in which Daniel Rudd's experience of *sensus fidelium* inspired and informed his leadership in the black Catholic community. Phelps discusses the Church's call to radical communion with "God, with all human beings, and with the universe" (p. 119).

She, like Gregory in the following section, discusses the problems of leadership and fragmentation in the black Catholic community, racism, women in ministry, evangelization, and building inclusive communities. A real highlight of this section is Hayes' "Faith of Our Mothers." In this paper Hayes challenges the biblical feminine ideal - meekness, subservience to men, lack of agency – and reveals biblical female strength. Hayes then describes the emergence of womanist theology and applies womanist readings of culture to the biblical representations of Eve, Mary Mother of Jesus, and Mary Magdelene. Finally, Massingale calls attention to the devastation of the HIV/AIDS pandemic and its impact on the African American population, and uses the lens of the black spirituals to understand the impact of this disease on black peoples and the larger community's relative indifference to the suffering it causes.

The *Pastoral Concerns* section opens with an essay by the Most Reverend Wilton D. Gregory, former President of the United States Conference of Catholic Bishops, who reminds us of how far African American Catholics have come, and points out several areas in which we must grow, such as leadership and youth ministry. Kevin Johnson's essay emphasizes the pivotal role that African American liturgical music plays in our ministries. Clarence Williams CPPS highlights the work of the National Black Catholic Clergy Caucus (NBCCC) in the development of a pan-African world view. Lastly, Paulinus Odozor CSSp describes the challenging experiences, even alienation, of African Catholic immigrants to the United States, jarringly reminiscent of those same challenges described in Jean K. Douglas' *Why I Left the*

Church, Why I Came Back, and Why I Just Might Leave Again (Fortuity Press 2006).

Uncommon Faithfulness is an essential work for Catholic theologians and scholars, no matter their cultural origins. As products of our cultures, it can be all too easy to become trapped in the prevailing prejudice and narrow-mindedness of our time. *Uncommon Faithfulness* reminds us that our opinions, beliefs, and habits shape our worlds, and presents the black Catholic experience as a model of faith, enlightenment, and perseverance in the face of injustice and oppression.

KIMBERLY B. FLINT-HAMILTON
DEPARTMENT OF SOCIOLOGY AND ANTHROPOLOGY
STETSON UNIVERSITY
DELAND, FL 32723

LaVergne, TN USA
01 October 2009
159537LV00002B/5/P